Fresh Water Aquarium Made Easy

Unlock Expert Tips, Brilliant Aquascape Ideas, and Beginner-Friendly Steps to Build a Healthy, Beautiful Aquarium

Luna Wildheart

Contents

Introduction

Get Ready to Dive In, Your Freshwater Aquarium Adventure Starts Here

So, you've taken the plunge. Maybe you already have a tank bubbling away in your living room, or maybe you're still staring at a box of equipment, wondering what goes where. Either way, congratulations, you're at the start of something fun, rewarding, and, yes, occasionally messy. But don't worry, you're not alone. This book is your buddy, your go-to guide, and maybe even your comic relief when the water turns cloudy and you're having a heartfelt talk with your filter. (Hey, we've all been there.)

I still remember setting up my very first aquarium. Watching those tiny, darting fish glide through plants and rocks felt like magic. But those early days also came with plenty of, "Wait... do I really need a water conditioner?" and, "Why is my fish giving me the side-eye?"

That's why I wrote this book. Because you don't need a marine biology degree or a thousand-dollar setup to build something beautiful. What you need is a guide that's clear, practical, and written by someone who's been in the deep end and lived to tell the tale.

Inside these pages, you'll find:

- Step-by-step help for setting up your first tank

- Tips for choosing fish and plants that actually get along

- Easy-to-follow advice on water care and equipment

- Solutions for the common oops moments, like that time I fed my fish a week's worth of food in one go

- A little humor, because we all need a laugh when our filter takes the day off

Whether 'you are 12 years old and dreaming of your first pet fish, or 60 and craving a relaxing hobby, this book is here to make the journey fun and stress-free.

This book won't overload you with technical jargon or assume you're ready to become a marine biologist. Instead, we'll walk step by step through the basics, help you troubleshoot like a pro, and most importantly, make fishkeeping feel fun. So take a deep breath, not in the tank please, flip the page, and get ready. You're not just building an aquarium, you are creating a tiny living world, and I can" wait to show you how.

Let's dive in.fun.

Chapter 1: Setting the Foundation: Choosing the Right Tank and Equipment

• • • • • • • • • •

Everything You Need to Know to Choose the Right Fish Tank, Equipment, and Budget-Friendly Setup Without the Guesswork

Ever tried fitting a square peg into a round hole? Setting up your first aquarium can feel just like that except in this case, the peg is a fish, and the hole is your living room. You might start out imagining a serene aquatic wonderland, complete with bubbling plants and graceful swimmers gliding past. But then reality kicks in. Where do you even start? What size tank should you get? Do fish really need all those gadgets? And why does your neighbor's tank look like an underwater interior decorator designed it, while yours resembles a murky science experiment?

Take a deep breath, friend. You're not alone.

This chapter is your compass. It's going to guide you through the choppy waters of choosing the right tank and equipment for your new aquatic adventure.

Understanding Aquarium Sizes: From Nano to Large Tanks

Let's start with tank size, because yes, size does matter (at least for fish tank size). Bigger isn't always better, but it makes things easier.

Imagine a 55-gallon tank, sprawling like an underwater metropolis. Fish roam free like teenagers at the mall, no curfew, no rules.Larger tanks come with an unexpected perk, *stability*. Just like your favorite pair of sweatpants, they're forgiving. That extra water volume helps dilute any mistakes, giving you more wiggle room to learn and grow without your fish staging a protest.

Now on the other end of the spectrum are nano tanks, those little tanks that are cute, compact, and surprisingly powerful. They're perfect if you don't have the spare the budget for a tank that rivals a coffee table. But here's the deal: small tanks require *more* attention. Like helicopter parent-level monitoring. A small shift in water chemistry can cause enormous problems fast. Still, for the detail-oriented aquarist, nano tanks are a satisfying challenge.

If you're just starting out, a 20-gallon tank might be your sweet spot. Not too big, not too small, just right. It's large enough to keep water conditions stable, but small enough to manage with no need for a forklift or a chemistry degree.

UNDERSTANDING AQUARIUM SIZES

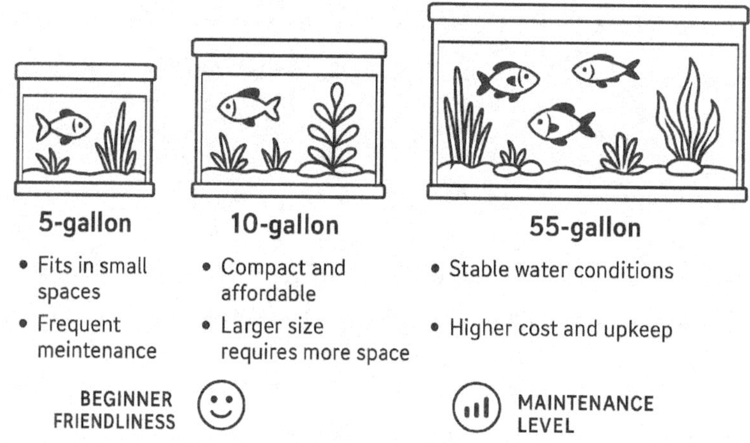

Tank sizes at a glance: From space-saving nano to majestic showstoppers.

Selecting the Perfect Tank: Material, Shape, and Space Considerations

Let's talk thanks not just how big, but *what kind*. Choosing the right tank material and shape can make a vast difference in how your aquarium looks, lasts, and fits into your space. It's kind of like picking out a sofa. You want it to be comfy, sturdy, and to match your vibe.

First, the material: glass or acrylic?

Glass is the old-school classic. It's strong, scratch-resistant, and won't discolor. Think of it as the dependable pickup truck of aquariums. It might be heavy, but it gets the job done without drama.The downside? If it cracks or chips, there's no fixing it. And lifting it feels like you're prepping for an Olympic deadlift.

Acrylic is the sleek sports car. Lightweight, clearer than glass, and more customizable. Want a round or corner tank? Acrylic is your best bet. But be careful, it scratches easier than a CD in a glove box. And some cleaners or chemicals can cloud it if you're not cautious. Still, if you want a unique look and easy handling, acrylic might be the way to go.

Now for tank shape. You've got more options than just a rectangle, although that's still the most beginner-friendly choice. Rectangular tanks are easy to clean, offer substantial surface area for oxygen exchange, and give fish plenty of horizontal swimming room.

Bow-front tanks have a gentle curve in the front glass that adds a sleek, modern feel and makes your aquascape pop like a museum display.Corner tanks? Great for tight spaces. They're space-saving and cozy, though they can be trickier to decorate.

Whatever shape you choose, make sure it fits your floor space literally. Measure your area, double-check where power outlets are, and think about where you'll do water changes. You'll also want to make sure your floor or stand can handle the weight. Remember, a gallon of water weighs over 8pounds. A 30-gallon tank? That's over 240 pounds, *before* you add substrate, decor, and gear.

And don't forget the aesthetics. Your tank shouldn't just be a home for fish, it can be a centerpiece in your room. Match the tank's style to your furniture. Want it to blend in? Go for a cabinet stand that hides cords and filters. Want it to stand out? Choose a sleek, rimless tank with a clean look and creative aquascape.

Long story short? Choose a tank that works with your lifestyle and space, not against it. You'll be happier, your fish will be happier, and your living room will thank you.

Essential Equipment: Filters, Heaters, and Lighting Explained

Now that you've got your tank picked out, it's time to talk gear. Think of this like setting up a little underwater apartment—your fish need clean air, comfy temperatures, and a light that says "home sweet home." Luckily, you don't need to spend a fortune or have a degree in engineering to get the basics right.

Filters–Your Tank's Heartbeat

A filter is your best friend. It keeps the water moving, removes waste, and gives beneficial bacteria a place to thrive. Without one, things get murky fast.

There are a few types of filters, but for most beginners, hang-on-back (HOB) filters are a significant starting point. They're easy to install, easy to clean, and don't take up much space inside the tank. Sponge environments like filters are also popular, especially for small tanks or gentle environments like betta setups and shrimp tanks. They run on air and are super gentle, great if you're worried about little fish being tossed around like laundry.

Canister filters are like the SUVs of filtration: powerful, quiet, and good for larger tanks. They sit outside the tank, which keeps things looking clean inside, but they take more effort to set up and maintain.

Ensure your chosen filter's rating suits your tank size or choose a slightly larger one. More filtration is usually better than less. Your fish will thank you for the fresh, flowing water.

Heaters–Keeping Things Toasty

Unless you live in the tropics or are keeping cold-water species like goldfish, you'll need a heater. Fish are sensitive to temperature changes, and consistent warmth is key to their health and happiness.

Most heaters are adjustable and submersible, meaning you position them in the water. Set it and forget it. A good rule of thumb is 3 to 5 watts per gallon of water. So for a 20-gallon tank, you'll want a heater between 75and 100 watts.

Be sure to place your heater where water flows freely near the filter outflow is perfect. That helps disperse the heat, so no fish ends up with the chills.

And yes, you'll also want a thermometer. Digital ones are easy to read, and some even alert you if the temperature drifts too far. A quick glance each day is all it takes to keep your fish cozy.

Lighting–More Than Just a Glow

Lighting does more than help you admire your beautiful tank.It also supports plant growth and keeps your fish on a natural day-night rhythm.

LED lights are the gold standard now. They are energy efficient, long-lasting, and don" heat up the water. Plus, many come with timers and even customizable color settings. Want a soft sunrise effect? You can do that. Want to spotlight your neon tetras like they're on stage? Totally doable.

If you have live plants, make sure your light supports plant growth. Look for full spectrum lighting that mimics natural sunlight.Otherwise, your plants will struggle, and algae may try to take over.

Budget-Friendly Tank Setups: Maximizing Quality without Breaking the Bank

Let's be real. Not everyone has hundreds of dollars to sink into a hobby, especially when you're just dipping your toes in. The good news? You absolutely *can* set up a gorgeous, thriving freshwater tank on a budget. It just takes a little planning, a sprinkle of creativity, and a few smart choices.

Start Small, but Not *Too* Small

It's tempting to grab one of those tiny desktop tanks, but they often end up being more trouble than they are worth. Small tanks are cheaper upfront, but harder to maintain and less forgiving when things go sideways..

A 10- to 20-gallon setup hits the sweet spot. You can often find starter kits that include a tank, filter, light, and even a heater all bundled together for less than buying each piece separately. These kits are perfect for beginners and often come with basic instructions to get you rolling.

Think Function first, Fancy Later

When you're budgeting, focus on function. You don't need high-end driftwood from some exotic riverbank or designer gravel to impress your fish—they couldn't careless.

Start with essential gear:

1. A decent filter

2. A reliable heater (if needed)
3. Simple substrates like gravel or sand
4. A thermometer
5. A test kit to check water quality (super important!)

Decorations? Get creative. Dollar stores often carry fake plants and glass gems that are safe at the aquarium. You can also use clean, untreated rocks or wood from outside. Just be sure to boil and test them first to make sure they're safe.

Choose Budget-Friendly Fish and Plants

Some fish are just more affordable than others. Guppies, plates, danios, white cloud minnows, and neon tetras are all colorful, hardy, and inexpensive. They're also choose budget peaceful and great for the community. Thanks.

Live plants can help keep your tank balanced and looking great, and they don" have to cost much. Try easy, budget-friendly species like:

- Java fern
- Anubias
- Hornwort
- Amazon sword
- Duckweed (free-floating and fast-growing)

Check local fish clubs or online aquarium groups—people often give away extra plants or sell them for just a couple of bucks.

Buy Secondhand(Smartly)

Check local classifieds, community groups, or fish forums. Many hobbyists sell gently used tanks and gear for a fraction of the original price. Just be sure to ask questions and inspect items for cracks, damage, or missing parts. A quick vinegar rinse can clean up most used equipment safely.

With a little patience and creativity, your aquarium doesn't need to cost a fortune. In fact, many experienced fish keepers will tell you their favorite setups were the ones built on a budget. Because when you work with what you have, you put more heart into every choice.

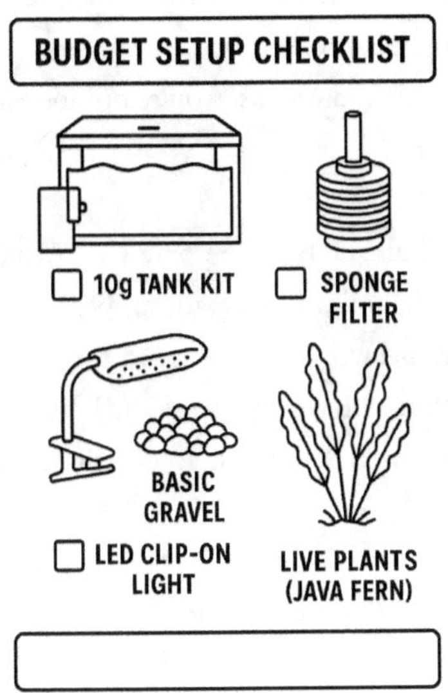

Smart spending = happy fish and happy wallet.

Sustainable Choices: Eco-friendly Equipment and Practices

Fish keeping is all about balance, and that doesn't just apply to water chemistry—it includes how we treat the planet too. A well-run freshwater tank can be beautiful and peaceful *and* sustainable, especially if you make a few thoughtful choices from the start.

Go LED All the Way

LED lighting isn't just sleek, it's energy efficient. These lights last longer, use less power, and don't overheat your tank like old-school bulbs. That means lower electric bills, less energy waste, and a safer environment for your fish and plants.

Many LED systems even come with timers or dimmers, helping you mimic a natural day-night cycle and reduce electricity use. It benefits everyone.

Save Water the Smart Way

Water changes are a must for healthy tanks, but they don't have to mean waste. Try these tips:

- Use old tank water to water your garden or houseplants. It's full of nutrients like nitrogen and phosphates. Plants love it.

- Only change what's needed. Most healthy tanks don't need a full water swap. Stick to 10 to 25 percent weekly unless something's gone off balance.
- Use a gravel vacuum. This helps you target debris and waste so you're not tossing out clean water by accident.

Choose Ethically Sourced Fish and Plants

Look for sellers who prioritize sustainability and humane breeding practices. Avoid fish that are wild, caught from endangered or fragile ecosystems. Instead, support local breeders or reputable online shops that care about animal welfare.

Some aquatic plants are invasive in the wild. Be careful with what you buy and how you dispose of extra trimmings. Never flush plants or fish down the drain. If you're trimming or re homing, do it responsibly.

Reduce, Reuse, Recycle (Fish keeper Style)

- **Reuse packaging.** Turn plant packaging into feeding trays or covers for tiny breeding tanks.

- **Repurpose containers.** Old food jars or plastic bins make great quarantine tanks or supply storage.

- **Recycle responsibly.** If you upgrade equipment, consider donating your old gear to schools, clubs, or beginner hobbyists.

Sustainability isn't about being perfect. It's about making little decisions that add up overtime. By being mindful of your resources and thoughtful in your purchases, you're not just building a fish tank, you're helping protect the bigger ecosystem too.

Avoiding Common Pitfalls: Equipment Failures and How to Prevent Them

Even the most well-meaning aquarist can hit a few snags along the way. And hey, that's part of the journey. But if I can help you dodge a few of the classic newbie mistakes, then your fish and your future self will both be grateful.

Mistake #1: Rushing the Process

We understand; you've set up the tank, the water looks good, and you're eager to add fish. But hold your bubbles! One of the biggest mistakes is skipping or rushing the cycling process. That's when beneficial bacteria build up to help handle fish waste. Without it, ammonia can spike and your fish can suffer.

Be patient. Let your tank cycle fully. Use water testing kits to track progress. If in doubt, wait it out. This part isn't glamorous, but it's what keeps your fish alive and happy long-term.

Mistake #2: Overfeeding

Fish always look hungry, but they're great at pretending. Too much food can lead to poor water quality and stressed-out fish. A good rule: feed only what your fish can eat in two minutes, once or twice a day.

And don't worry if they skip a meal now and then. A little fasting can be healthy for them.

Mistake #3: Skipping Water Tests

Guessing isn't a strategy. Water might look clean but still be unbalanced. Test your water regularly for ammonia, nitrite, nitrate, and pH levels. Knowing your numbers means you can catch issues before they become disasters.

Water test kits are a small investment with big payoffs and they make you feel like a science wizard.

Mistake #4: Cleaning Everything Too Well

You want a clean tank, sure, but don't scrub away all that good bacteria living in your filter and decorations. Avoid using soap or bleach unless it's absolutely necessary and always rinse with dechlorinated water.

A little alga is normal. Think of it like a tank character.

Mistake #5: Too Many Fish, Too Fast

It's easy to get carried away at the pet store. So many colors! So many cute little faces! But adding too many fish too quickly can overload your biological filter and cause stress or illness.

Start small, stock gradually, and research compatibility. Your tank should be a peaceful little underwater community, not a fishy free-for-all.

Final Tip? Learn, Adjust, and Have Fun.

Every aquarist makes a mistake at some point. What matters is that you *learn*, adjust, and keep. This hobby is all about the balance between science and art, between patience and excitement, between clean tanks and fish with attitude.

You are doing great just by reading this and taking it one step at a time.

A beginner-friendly freshwater tank: clear water, soft lighting, thriving plants, and happy fish—everything starts with a solid setup.

Chapter 2:
Aquascaping Artistry: Craft Visually Beautiful Underwater Worlds

• • • • • • • • • • •

Designing Show-Stopping Underwater Landscapes with Rocks, Plants, and Creative Layering Techniques

S uppose you walk into a room and sea tank that takes your breath away, not because it smells like fish, but because it looks like a meticulously crafted piece of art.

Aquascaping is where creativity meets aquatic life, transforming your basic tank into a stunning underwater masterpiece. It's like painting, but your canvas is full of water, and your paints are living, breathing, plants and rocks.

This chapter guides you through the essentials of aquascaping, allowing you to create a captivating tank that even your fish will stop and stare at.

What's included:

* **Balance, Depth, and Focal Points**

* **Layering like a movie set** (foreground to background and golden)

* **Layout styles** like the Rule of Thirds and Golden Ratio

* **Plant and hardscape placement** tips for drama and calm

* **Practical setup tips** to avoid the muddy middle

Principles of Aquascaping: Balance, Depth, and Focal Points

Creating Depth and Drama

Principles of Varying plant height and texture enhances the feeling of depth, turning your tank into a lush underwater jungle rather than a flat landscape. Use plants with different leaf shapes and sizes to add complexity and intrigue.

Let's talk about the focal points. The stars of your aquatic stage. A focal point draws the eye like a lighthouse in the sea. It could be a striking rock, a boldly colored plant, or a fun piece of driftwood. Contrast is the secret sauce. Try a red plant in a sea of green, or one large stone surrounded by smaller ones to guide the viewer's gaze and keep them mesmerized.

Different aquascaping styles bring these principles to life. Zen-inspired designs use simple layouts with just a few elements, creating a peaceful, clutter-free atmosphere. Think of it like the Marie Kondo of aquascaping—only what sparks joy gets to stay.

On the other end of the spectrum, jungle-style aquascapes go big and bold. They're packed with dense plant growth, layers of texture, and a wild mix of colors. It's like a rainforest in your living room.

Case Study: Jamie's First Aquascape

Jamie, a creative 15-year-old, transformed a plain tank into a vibrant underwater forest. By using the Rule of Thirds and a punch of color, Jamie made a striking red plant for the star. Layering plants of different sizes and shapes gave the tank depth and energy. The result? A tiny jungle with big personality and proof that anyone can make aquascaping magic happen with a little guidance and imagination.

Hardscape Elements: Choosing and Arranging Rocks and Driftwood

Picture this: you're staring at a pile of rocks and driftwood, wondering how on earth to transform this mess into something gallery-worthy. Fear not! These natural elements are your secret weapons in crafting a breathtaking aquascape.

Rocks add structure and shape. They're the bones of your design. Driftwood brings texture and depth ,it's the muscle. Together, they form the landscape of your underwater world, creating a scene that mimics rivers, streams, or forest floors. And your fish? They'll love the nooks and crannies for exploring, hiding, and playing territorial games.

But not all rocks and wood are fish tank safe. Choose wisely. Use Seiryu stone or dragon rock, both aquarium-friendly and beautiful. For driftwood, Malaysian and Manzanita are reliable favorites. They even release natural tannins that soften water and give your tank a cozy, authentic look.

Avoid rocks that fizz in vinegar (hello, calcium overload!) and steer clear of toxic wood like cedar or walnut.

Now for the fun part arranging your hardscape. Think naturally, not a row of soldier stones. Use odd numbers (three or five rocks, never four!) to create visual harmony. Cluster and layer pieces to build height and depth and always check for stability. You don't want a mini landslide in your tank when your corydora goes exploring.

*A gently sloped base and layers of plant height create
the illusion of depth, like a miniature riverscape.*

Plant selection: Matching Flora to Your Aquascape Design

First Let's Anchor Your Vision

Driftwood is beautiful, but it can float like a stubborn pool noodle if you don't secure it. Use fishing line or aquarium-safe glue to anchor your pieces in place. This lets you build sweeping, stable structures that stay put and look natural.

Now blend your hardscape and plant life. This is where the magic really happens.

Let mosses like Java Moss creep over wood, adding softness and mystery. Pair Anubias or Java Fern with rocks to create contrast, lush greenery spilling over rough stone. It's functional, too. These cozy corners give fish places to hide, helping them feel secure and at home.

Now let's move onto Plant selection: Matching Flora to Your Aquascape Design.

Standing in the aquatic plant aisle can feel like a jungle in itself. Don't panic, we've all been there.

Think of low-maintenance plants as the sweatpants of the plant world: comfy, reliable, and forgiving. These are your Anubias, Java ferns, and Amazon Swords, perfect for beginners or busy fish parents.

Then you've got the high-maintenance glam squad. Dwarf Hairgrass, Rotala, or Monte Carlo demand good lighting, CO2, and nutrients, but reward you with show-stopping style.

Mix up colors and textures. Try combining light and dark green, long grassy strands with broad leaves. It's like decorating a living room with rootshroots.

.Creating Depth: Layering Techniques for a 3D Effect

Visualize peering into your aquarium and feeling like you could just step inside and wander through an underwater forest. That's the magic of depth in aquascaping—a trick of the eye that transforms a flat tank into a three-dimensional wonderland. Layering is your secret weapon here, using strategic plant and hardscape placement to create the illusion of depth. Think of your tank as a stage where plants and rocks play the lead roles. By overlapping these elements, you add visual interest and complexity. Place taller plants behind shorter ones, and nestle larger rocks in front of smaller ones. This creates a sense of layering, drawing the eye deeper into the scene. It's like stacking pancakes but without sticky syrup. Using perspective is another clever tool. Arrange elements to guide the viewer's eye, creating pathways and focal points that invite exploration.

But wait, there's more! The illusion of distance can take your aquascape to the next level. Shrinking plant sizes as you move toward the back of the tank is a neat trick. It makes the space seem larger than it is, like a magician's sleight of hand. By placing smaller plants in the background, you create a sense of vastness, turning your tank into an endless underwater expanse. Color gradients can also play a part. Use lighter colors in the foreground and darker shades in the back to enhance the perception of depth. It's like painting a landscape with watercolors. Subtle shifts in hue create a multi-dimensional dynamic duo effect.

Now, let's talk about shadows and light—nature's dynamic duo. Proper lighting can work wonders in enhancing the 3D effect of your aquascape. Highlight specific areas with focused lighting, drawing attention to key features and creating dramatic contrasts. This technique is like shining a spotlight on the star of the show, ensuring they get the attention they deserve. Shadows, too, can add depth and intrigue. By strategically placing hardscape elements, you can cast interesting shadows that dance across the substrate, adding an element of mystery. It's like a shadow puppet show for fish, keeping them entertained and engaged.

For those seeking inspiration, look no further than nature itself. Riverbeds and forests offer perfect examples of natural layering, with elements overlapping Biotope aquascapes aim to recreate specific natural environments, using plants and materials native to a particular region. For example, a South American setup might feature Amazon Swords and Java Ferns, while an Asian-themed tank could highlight Anubias and Java Moss. These tanks don't just look beautiful, but mirrors their natural home. The right plants not only complete the visual but contribute to a thriving ecosystem. Whether you're going for a lush jungle or a tranquil stream, plant choice brings your aquascape to life in both form and function.

Creating the illusion of depth can truly transform a tank. By strategically layering your plants and rocks, you guide the viewer's eye through could almost a scene that feels immersive and multidimensional. Tall plants in the back, shorter ones in front. This simple trick makes all the difference. Use larger rocks in the foreground and shrink plant sizes toward the back to make the space feel larger than it really is. Layering and perspective techniques are subtle, but they turn a flat layout into a tiny world you could almost step into. It's not magic, it's aquascaping.

Layering and interweaving to create complexity and depth. Emulate these scenes by arranging your aquascape in layers, using rocks and wood to mimic the contours of a riverbed or the tangled roots of a forest. The result is a captivating, immersive environment that draws viewers in and invites them to explore each nook and cranny.

Inspired Design: A Step-by-Step Guide to Layering

Creating a stunning aquascape isn't just about choosing beautiful plants and decorations—it's about designing with depth and perspective in mind. One of the easiest ways to bring your aquascape to life is by mastering layering. Layering turns a flat tank into a three-dimensional underwater world that feels natural, balanced, and dynamic.

Here's how you can achieve this effect step by step.

Step 1: Build Your Foundation with Substrate

Start by adding substrate—this can be aquarium soil, gravel, or sand.

- Slope the substrate from front to back.

  - We should build the front higher, creating a gentle slope.

    ○ This slope could have a thin layer.

- The back shows the illusion of depth, much like a hiking trail that winds toward the hills in the distance.

Pro Tip: Pack the back slope firmly so it doesn't collapse.

Step 2: Place Your hardscape Elements

With your sloped base in place, it's time to add rocks and driftwood (your hardscape). This is where you build the structure of your aquascape.

- Place larger rocks or wood toward the front to make them appear closer to the viewer.

- Use smaller stones or thinner branches toward the back to give the illusion that they're far away.

- Arrange them so they seem naturally placed, not too symmetrical or evenly spaced.

Pro Tip: Try tilting stones or placing wood at different angles to create a sense of movement and natural flow.

Step 3: Layer Your plants for a Natural Look

Now it's time to add plants to bring life and color to your scene.

- Place short, carpet-like plants such as Dwarf Hairgrass or Monte Carlo in the foreground.

- Mid-sized plants, like Cryptocoryne or Java Fern, go in the middle layers.

- Taller plants, such as Vallisneria or Amazon Sword, belong at the back to frame your design.

This layering of plant heights adds both depth and texture, making your aquascape feel like a miniature world.

Step 4: Use Lighting to Highlight Your Design

Lighting plays a key role in focusing attention and enhancing depth.

- Angle your lights or adjust their position to highlight specific areas, such as your main rock or a cluster of plants.

- Consider using spotlight effects or dimmer settings to create shadows and contrast, giving your tank a more dramatic three-dimensional appearance.

Pro Tip: Avoid flat, even lighting across the entire tank, as it can reduce the sense of depth.

Step 5: Step Back and Evaluate

After placing everything, step back and view your aquascape from different angles.

- Does it feel balanced?

- Does your eye naturally follow the layout from front to back?

Is there a clear focal point, or centerpiece? Make minor adjustments as needed until the design feels right to you.

Your Aquarium, Your Masterpiece

Remember, layering is part art and part technique. Don't be afraid to experiment, move elements around, and try new combinations. With patience and creativity, you'll transform your aquarium into a living, breathing 3D masterpiece that draws attention and sparks imagination.

Happy aquascaping!

A gently sloped base and layers of plant height create the illusion of depth like a miniature riverscape.

Maintaining Plant Health: CO2 and Nutrient Management

Master the nitrogen cycle, testing, and water balance to keep fish happy and water healthy.

Ever walked into a room and felt like you're breathing through a damp sock? Welcome to the world of poor water chemistry. In aquariums, water chemistry is the lifeline for your fishy pals. It's like being on a diet of pizza and ice cream—it sounds fun at first, but it's not sustainable. Fish need water that's just right, like Goldilocks' porridge. If things are off, even by a little, you could end up with a tank full of grumpy fish giving you the side-eye.

Understanding water chemistry might sound like a task for a lab coat-wearing scientist, but fear not. With a bit of guidance, you'll be navigating pH levels and ammonia like a pro.

Let's look at the nitrogen cycle, the backbone of aquarium health

What is the nitrogen cycle? It is the unsung hero of your aquarium. It's the backstage crew that keeps the show running smoothly while your fish plays with the stars.

Think of it as a three-step dance: ammonia, nitrite, nitrate. When you feed your fish, and they do their business, waste builds up and releases ammonia, which is toxic enough to make your fish feel like they've harmful substance been swimming in a soup of doom.

Enter stage right: nitrifying bacteria. These little champs convert ammonia into nitrite, which spoiler alert is still toxic. But fear not. Another set of bacteria transforms nitrite into nitrate, a less harmful substance that fish can tolerate in small amounts. Regular water changes are your best friend here, helping to keep nitrate levels in check and your fish in their happy place.

Starting a new aquarium is like inviting the nitrogen cycle to a party. But first, you've got to set the stage.

Troubleshooting Common Aquascaping Problems: Algae and Plant decay

Fishless cycling is a popular method, allowing you to establish this bacterial army without risking your fish's well-being. It involves adding a source of ammonia to the tank—like a pinch of fish food or bottled ammonia product. Over time, beneficial bacteria colonize your filter and substrate, transforming ammonia to nitrite and then to nitrate. You can also use bottled starter bacteria to speed up the process, kind of like hiring a DJ to jumpstart the aquarium party.

You can recognize a fully cycled tank the same way you recognize a perfectly baked cake. When your ammonia and nitrite levels drop to zero, and you're seeing a steady rise in nitrates, you're ready. That's your green light to welcome your fishy friends.

Beware: New Tank Syndrome results from adding fish too soon. This is when your water still holds ammonia and nitrite, and your fish are the unwilling test subjects. Look out for signs like clamped fins, hiding, or general "not feeling it" energy. The solution? Patience. Let the cycle complete before anyone moves in.

Things don't always go as planned. A stalled cycle might mean your bacteria got wiped out by over-cleaning or untreated tap water. If that happens, add more bacteria and reduce disruptions—like inviting more guests to keep the party vibe alive. If ammonia levels spike, it might be from overfeeding. Try small water changes and easing up on the food. Cycling takes time, but when done right, it's the invisible superhero behind every thriving tank.

Chapter 3: Water Chemistry Demystified: Maintaining a Healthy Aquarium Environment

• • • ● • ● ● ● • •

Master the Nitrogen Cycle, Testing, and Water Balance to Keep Fish Happy and Water Healthy

Ever walked into a room and felt like you're breathing through a damp sock? Welcome to the world of poor water chemistry! In aquariums, water chemistry is the lifeline for your fishy pals. It's like being on a diet of pizza and ice cream—sounds fun at first, but not sustainable. Fish need water that's just right, like Goldilocks' porridge. If it's off, even by a little, you could end up with a tank full of grumpy fish giving you the side-eye. Understanding water chemistry might sound like a task for a lab coat-wearing scientist, but fear not! With a bit of guidance, you'll be navigating pH levels and ammonia like a pro.

The Nitrogen Cycle: Understanding the Backbone of Aquarium Health

Let's talk about the nitrogen cycle, the unsung hero of your aquarium. It's the backstage crew who keeps the show running smoothly while your fish plays with the stars. Think of it as a three-step dance: ammonia, nitrite, nitrate. When you feed your fish, and they do their business, waste builds up, releasing ammonia, which is toxic enough to make your fish feel like they've been swimming in a toxic soup. Enter stage right: nitrifying bacteria. These little champs convert ammonia into nitrite, which, spoiler alert, is still toxic. But fear not, because another set of bacteria transforms nitrite into nitrate, a less harmful substance that fish can tolerate in small amounts. Regular water changes are your best friend here, helping keep nitrate levels in check and ensuring your fish stay happy and healthy.

Starting a new aquarium is like inviting the nitrogen cycle to a party, but you've got to set the stage first. In a new tank, beneficial bacteria are like guests waiting for an invitation. To kick things off, you need to cycle your tank, preparing it for the nitrogen cycle like setting up the ultimate aquarium rave. Fishless cycling is a popular method, allowing you to establish this bacterial army without risking your fish's well-being. It involves adding a source of ammonia to the tank, like fish food or a bottled ammonia product. Over time, bacteria will colonize your filter and substrate, transforming ammonia to nitrite and then to nitrate. You can also use starter bacteria products to speed up this process, much like adding a DJ to get the party started.

Understanding a healthy nitrogen cycle is akin to recognizing the perfect baking point of a cake. When ammonia and nitrite levels hit zero, and you notice a gradual buildup of nitrates, your aquarium is ready for its fishy inhabitants. A stable nitrogen cycle is the green light for adding fish, much like a bouncer giving you the nod at the club entrance. But beware the dreaded New Tank Syndrome! This occurs when you add fish too soon, subjecting them to unprocessed ammonia and nitrite. Symptoms include fish hiding, clamped fins, and even the grim reaper showing up uninvited. Avoid it by cycling your tank thoroughly before introducing any fishy friends.

Even the best-laid plans can hit a bump, and the nitrogen cycle is no exception. A stalled cycle can occur because of insufficient bacteria, often caused by over-cleaning or harsh tap water treatments. Remedy this by adding more bacteria—think of it as inviting extra party guests to keep things lively. High ammonia levels during cycling can result from too much food or overcrowding. Manage this by performing partial water changes and reducing food. Remember, patience is key. Cycling can take several weeks, but once complete, your tank will be a thriving aquatic paradise.

Interactive Element: Nitrogen Cycle Checklist

The nitrogen cycle is the hidden superhero of every healthy aquarium. It keeps the water safe by breaking down fish waste and leftover food into less harmful substances. Use this easy checklist to kick-start and manage the nitrogen cycle before adding fish to your tank.

Step-by-Step Nitrogen Cycle Checklist

Step 1: Start with a Source of Ammonia

Add fish food, pure ammonia, or another ammonia source to kick-start the cycle. This feeds the beneficial bacteria that will soon grow in your tank.

Step 2: Test Your Water Weekly

Use a water test kit to check for:

- Ammonia

- Nitrite

- Nitrate

Keep testing once a week to track the progress of your cycle.

Step 3: Wait for Ammonia and Nitrite to Reach Zero

Be patient! Your cycle is ready when ammonia and nitrite levels drop to zero, and nitrate levels rise slightly. This shows that beneficial bacteria are doing their job.

Step 4: Perform Partial Water Changes

Do partial water changes to keep nitrate levels in a safe range? This helps prevent stress or harm to your fish once they're added.

Step 5: Add Fish Slowly

Introduce just a few fish at a time to avoid overwhelming the system. This gives your tank time to adjust and keeps your fish safe and healthy.

Congratulations!

With this checklist, you're ready to manage your aquarium" water chemistry like a pro. Remember, a stable nitrogen cycle keeps your fish happy, healthy, and swimming in crystal-clear water.

Testing Water Parameters: Tools and Techniques for Accuracy

Step-by-Step Nitrogen Cycle Checklist

Step 1: Start with a Source of Ammonia

Add fish food, pure ammonia, or another ammonia source to kick-start the cycle. This feeds the beneficial bacteria that will soon grow in your tank.

Step 2: Test Your Water Weekly.

Use Changes to do a water test kit to check for ammonia, nitrite, and nitrate. Keep testing once a week to track the progress of your cycle.

Step 3: Wait for Ammonia and Nitrite to Reach Zero

Be patient! Your cycle is ready when ammonia and nitrite levels drop to zero, and nitrate levels rise slightly. That means the bacteria are doing their job.

Step 4: Perform Partial Water Changes.

Do partial water changes to keep nitrate levels in a safe range. This helps prevent stress or harm to your fish once they're added.

Step 5: Add Fish Slowly.

Introduce just a few fish at a time to avoid overwhelming the system. This gives your tank time to adjust and keeps your fish safe and healthy.

Congratulations!

With this checklist, you're ready to manage your aquarium water chemistry like a pro.

A multi-stage filtration system helps remove waste, support beneficial bacteria, and keep your water safe.

Testing Water Parameters: Tools and Techniques for Accuracy

Picture this: your fish are like tiny, scaly canaries in a coal mine, swimming around, blissfully unaware of the potential chaos lurking in their watery world. Regular water testing is your secret weapon, your way of ensuring that everything in the tank is copacetic and your fish doesn't start a mutiny.

It's the best way to catch imbalances before they turn your serene aquarium into a scene from a disaster movie. By keeping tabs on parameters like ammonia, nitrite, nitrate, and pH, you're basically acting as the tank's personal life coach—steering it clear of an existential crisis. And when you track those readings over time? You're not just reacting; you're predicting. Like an aquarium psychic.

Visual Element: Water Testing Routine Chart

Keeping your aquarium water safe isn't a onetime task, it's an ongoing routine that helps prevent fish stress, illness, and algae outbreaks. This Water Testing Routine Chart helps you track your water parameters consistently, so you always know when your aquarium needs attention.

How to Use This Chart

1.**Hang the chart near your aquarium** or keep it in your aquarium care journal.

2.**Testy our water** using a liquid test kit or test strips.

3.Record your **results** in the chart each week and month.

4.**Review the trends** to spot any changes or problems early.

Key Water Parameters to Test

- Ammonia (NH_3/NH_4^+):

o   Should stay at **0 ppm**. High levels are toxic to fish.

- Nitrite (NO_2^-):

o   Should stay at **0 ppm**. High levels can cause breathing problems.

- Nitrate (NO_3^-):

o   Should stay **below 40 ppm**. High levels can stress fish and fuel algae.

- pH (Acidity/Alkalinity):

o   Most freshwater fish thrive between **6.5 and 7.5**. Stability is key.

- Water Hardness (GH/KH):

o   Important for maintaining stable pH and fish health.

- Temperature:

o   Keep stable based on your fish species, usually **72°F to 78°F (22°C to 26°C)**.

Sample Water Testing Routine Chart

On a grid sheet, label the columns with:

Date, Ammonia (ppm), Nitrite (ppm), Nitrate (ppm), pH, GH/KH, Temp (°F/°C), Notes

Week 1   Week 2   Week 3   Week 4   Monthly

Why Track Your Results?

- Spot problems early before they harm your fish.
- Maintain a healthy cycle by preventing ammonia or nitrite spikes.
- Prevent algae by keeping nitrates in check.
- Ensure stable conditions for stress-free, lucky fish.

Pro Tip:

Create the chart, laminate it, and use a dry-erase marker to update it weekly. This way, you can reuse it month after month!

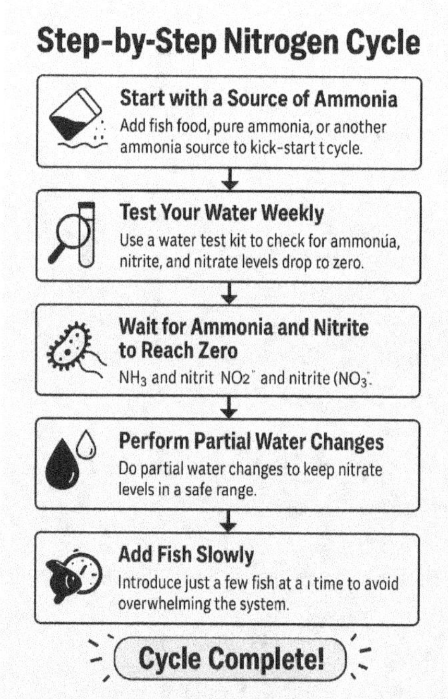

The nitrogen cycle converts ammonia (NH_3) to nitrite (NO_2-), then to nitrate (NO_3-). This process is the biological backbone of a healthy aquarium.

Adjusting pH and Hardness: Tailoring Water Conditions for Your Fish

Picture your aquarium as a bustling, underwater city. Just like any city, it thrives on balance and harmony, and a big part of that harmony comes down to pH and water hardness. These might sound like scientific buzzwords, but they're crucial for keeping your fish population happy and healthy. Each fish species has its own preference for pH, which is a measure of how acidic or alkaline the water is. Think of pH as the Goldilocks factor, not too high, not too low, but just right. For instance, most freshwater fish like a pH range of 6.5 to 7.5. Discuss, those beautifully round and colorful fish, prefer a slightly acidic environment around 6.0 to 6.5. Meanwhile, African Cichlids are the rebels of the fish world, thriving in alkaline waters with a pH of 7.5 to 8.5. Water hardness refers to the concentration of minerals in the water, like calcium and magnesium. Some fish, like livebearers, thrive in harder waters, while others, such as tetras and rasboras, prefer softer waters.Tailoring these conditions to suit your fish is like giving them a customized home makeover, ensuring they thrive in their watery abode.

Now, if your pH is off kilter, don't panic! Adjusting it is a bit like tweaking a recipe, adding a pinch of this or that until it's just right. If you need to raise the pH, you might use buffers. These are like little guardians that keep your pH steady, even when outside forces try to tip the balance. On the flip side, if you need to lower the pH, natural methods can be your best friend. Driftwood, for example, releases tannins that naturally lower pH levels. It's like adding a dash of lemon juice to a salad—simple yet effective. Catappa leaves, or Indian Almond leaves, also help reduce pH while adding a touch of authenticity to your tank. Just avoid rapid changes, as sudden swings can stress your fish more than a surprise pop quiz.

You can also adjust water hardness, albeit with a bit more finesse. If your water is too soft, adding minerals is a straightforward approach. Products like crushed coral or limestone can accumulate hardness, much like adding a sprinkle of salt to your cooking. If you need to soften your water, reverse osmosis (RO) systems are your go-to. These systems filter out excess minerals, giving you pure, soft water. It's like running your water through a spa treatment, leaving it refreshed and revitalized. However, it's important to remember that consistency is key. Fish are creatures of habit, and they appreciate stable conditions. So, when making any changes, do it gradually to avoid turning your aquarium into a rollercoaster ride for your fish.

Different fish have different needs, and understanding these needs is like having a cheat sheet for a successful aquarium. Take Discus, for example. They hail from the soft, acidic waters of the Amazon Basin. To keep them in tip-top shape, aim for soft water with a low pH, using RO water to achieve this if necessary. African Cichlids come from the hard, alkaline waters of the African rift lakes. They thrive in tanks with higher pH and hardness levels, and adding limestone or coral can help recreate their natural environment. Biotope tanks, which mimic natural habitats, can be a rewarding way to cater to these preferences. Imagine setting up a South American biotope for your Discus, with driftwood, tannin-rich waters, and lush plant growth. Or create an African lake biotope for your Cichlids with rocky substrates and hard water. These setups not only enhance fish health but also bring a slice of the wild into your home.

Addressing Ammonia Spikes: Causes and Solutions

Envision your fish living in a world where the air suddenly becomes toxic, and you'll get a sense of what an ammonia spike feels like for them. It's like someone threw a party and forgot to take out the trash for weeks. One moment, everything's peaceful and serene, and the next, your fish are gasping for breath like they've just run a marathon. So, what causes these ammonia spikes? Often, it's the result of overfeeding. You might think you're being generous, giving your fish that extra pinch of food, but what you're really doing is creating a buffet of uneaten food that decays and releases ammonia. It's the fishy equivalent of a fast-food binge gone wrong. Then there's inadequate filtration. If your filter isn't up to snuff, it can't process all the waste, leading to a build-up that spikes ammonia levels. And let's not forget the tragic case of bacterial die-off, where the helpful bacteria that usually keep ammonia in check decide to take a vacation, leaving your fish in atoxic soup.

When you notice an ammonia spike, it's time to spring into action faster than a cat spotting a laser pointer. First, perform a partial water change. This is your go-to emergency measure, like calling in the cavalry. Replacing a portion of the water helps dilute the ammonia, giving your fish some much-needed relief. You can also use ammonia-absorbing products, which act like sponges, soaking up the offending chemical and making the water safe again. It's akin to using a mop on a spill—quick, and a lifesaver in a pinch.

For long-term peace of mind, prevention is key. Proper feeding practices are your first line of defense. Feed your fish only for what they can consume in a few minutes and resist the urge to offer seconds. Think of it as portion control for your fishy friends. Regular filter maintenance is also crucial. Clean your filter media regularly, but avoid over-cleaning, which can wipe out beneficial bacteria. Remember, these bacteria are your best allies, breaking down waste and keeping ammonia levels stable. They're like the unsung heroes of the aquarium world, working behind the scenes to ensure everything runs smoothly.

Now, how do you spot the signs of ammonia stress in your fish? Picture a fish gasping at the surface, looking like it's auditioning fora role in an underwater drama. That's a classic sign. Your fish might also show red or inflamed gills, which are essentially their way of crying out for help.If you notice these symptoms, it's time to put on your detective hat and check for ammonia levels. Catching it early can make all the difference, turning a potential disaster into a minor hiccup in your aquarium management.

Addressing ammonia spikes involves a mix of vigilance, quick action, and preventative strategies. By understanding the causes and knowing how to respond, you can keep your aquarium a haven for your fish rather than a hazardous zone. Remember, a healthy tank is a happy tank, and with a little attention to detail, you can ensure your aquatic friends thrive in their underwater abode.

Water Changes: Frequency, Techniques, and Benefits

Picture this: your aquarium is like a bustling underwater city, teeming with fishy residents going about their daily lives. Just as a city needs sanitation workers to keep it clean, your tank needs regular water changes to stay fresh and healthy. Think of water changes as hitting the refresh button on your aquarium, removing waste and toxins that accumulate.Fish waste, uneaten food, and decaying plant material can turn your crystal-clear water into a murky mess faster than you can say "fish fry."By performing regular water changes, you effectively remove these pollutants, preventing them from reaching levels that could harm your finned friends. But that's not all—water changes also replenish essential minerals and nutrients that support fish health and plant growth. It's like giving your tank a vitamin boost, ensuring your fish remain vibrant.

How often should you work on things? The frequency of water changes depends on your tank's setup and bio load. For community tanks, where multiple species coexist, aim for a weekly water change of 20-30%. This keeps the water quality high and the environment stable, much like a weekly cleaning routine in your home. For low-bio load setups, where fewer fish call your tank home, bi-weekly changes may suffice. It's all about finding the balance that suits your tank's unique needs. Regular testing of water parameters can help you determine the ideal schedule, ensuring your aquatic residents thrive without unnecessary stress.

When it's time to perform a water change, efficiency is key.Gravel vacuums are your best friends, allowing you to remove debris from the substrate while siphoning out the old water. It's like vacuuming your livingroom while mopping the floor at the same time—a multitasker's dream! As you siphon, watch the gravel closely, letting the vacuum do its magic in removing waste without disturbing the substrate too much. Meanwhile, prepare your replacement water to match the tank's conditions, ensuring the temperature, pH, and hardness are like what's already in your aquarium. This minimizes the shock to your fish, changing as smooth as a fish gliding through water.

Fish are sensitive souls, easily stressed by sudden changes. To minimize their anxiety during water changes, gradual adjustments are crucial. When adding fresh water, ensure it's at a similar temperature to what's already in the tank. Double-check the temperature with a thermometer to avoid subjecting your fish to a mini ice age or tropical heatwave. Try to keep noise and vibrations to a minimum. Fish aren't fans of rock concerts, so avoid banging equipment around or creating unnecessary disturbances. Quiet operations help maintain a calm environment, allowing your fish to continue their aquatic ballet undisturbed.

Water changes are more than just a mundane chore—they're a vital part of aquarium maintenance that keeps your tank looking its best. By following these guidelines and making water changes a regular part of your routine, you'll ensure a healthy, thriving environment for your aquatic companions. Your fish will thank you with their vibrant colors and playful antics, turning your tank into a stunning centerpiece that brings joy to your home.

Sustainable Water Practices: Conservation and Waste Reduction

Ever thought your aquarium could help save the planet? Well, maybe not single-handedly, but every little drop counts for water conservation. You might not realize it, but aquariums can gulp down water faster than a marathon runner at the finish line. The good news is, by adopting some savvy water-saving practices, you can reduce your tank's thirstiness and become an eco-warrior at the same time. Let's start with the basics: reducing water waste. It's like teaching your tank to sip rather than guzzle. Instead of blasting your way through gallons during maintenance, consider using a more measured approach. Rainwater collection is a nifty trick, offering a natural, chemical-free alternative for water changes. Just make sure to filter it to avoid any unwanted surprises, like leaves or the odd bug, unless your fish fancy a snack.

Water-saving devices are another ace up your sleeve. Think of them as the gadgetry of the aquarium world, designed to trim down your tank's water use. For instance, you can install flow structures on your faucets, ensuring you don't waste more water than necessary when filling your tank. It's like putting your tank on a diet—less waste, more efficiency. And if you're feeling tech-savvy, programmable timers can manage water changes with precision, ensuring you don't accidentally flood your living room while you're engrossed in the latest episode of your favorite show.

And let's not forget about minimizing chemical use. Your tank doesn't need to be a chemistry lab to stay healthy. Encouraging biological filtration is like hiring Mother Nature as your personal water quality manager.Beneficial bacteria can handle waste better than most chemical additives, keeping your tank's ecosystem in balance. Meanwhile, plants are the unsung heroes of natural filtration. They absorb nutrients directly from the water, reducing the need for chemical interventions. It's like having a team of tiny gardeners working around the clock, ensuring your tank stays pristine and your fish remain happy.

Eco-friendly aquarists are leading the charge, showing that sustainable practices can make a big splash. Take, for example, the aquarists who have embraced closed-loop systems. These setups recycle water within the tank, minimizing waste and making every drop count. Picture a zero-waste aquarium; we filter and reuse the water, creating a self-sustaining ecosystem.It's like the ultimate recycling project, right in your living room. And then there are those who have taken the plunge into completely chemical-free tank s.By relying on nature's own filtration methods, they've maintained stunning aquariums that are as kind to the planet as they are to the fish.

Incorporating sustainable practices isn't just about reducing your environmental footprint—it's about enhancing the quality of life of your aquatic companions. By conserving water, minimizing chemicals, and embracing natural solutions, you create a healthier environment for your fish and a more rewarding experience for yourself. So, think of your aquarium not just as a hobby, but as a tiny aquatic ambassador, helping you make a positive impact on the world around you. As we wrap up this chapter on water chemistry, remember that each choice you make contributes to a greater good. Now, with a solid understanding of sustainable practices, you're ready to explore the fascinating world of aquarium ecosystems in the next chapter.

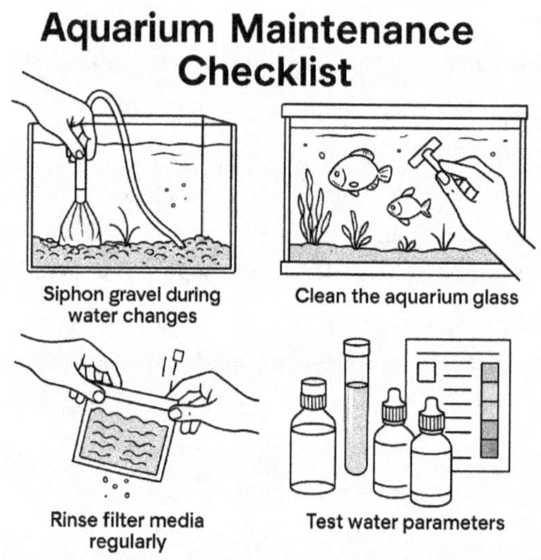

Basic weekly maintenance tasks like testing water, rinsing filters, and cleaning gravel help keep your aquarium clean, clear, and stress-free for your fish.

Chapter 4: Stocking Your Aquarium: Fish Compatibility and Behavior

How to Choose Compatible Fish, Prevent Stress, and Build a Peaceful Aquatic Community

Suppose you're throwing a party, but instead of guests with questionable dance moves, you've got fish with even more questionable swimming patterns. You're the host, and your tank is on the dance floor. The goal? To avoid the underwater equivalent of a mosh pit. Welcome to the world of stocking your aquarium, where choosing the right fish is as crucial as picking the perfect playlist for a party. You want a harmonious blend, fish that get along swimmingly and don't start a brawl over the last flake of fish food. In this chapter, we'll explore the ins and outs of selecting fish that won't just survive but thrive together, bringing your tank to life with color and movement.

Starting with the rock stars of the beginner world, let's talk about Zebra Danios. These striped speedsters are the marathon runners of the fish world, renowned for their adaptability to various conditions. Whether the water's chilly or your heater's on the fritz, Zebra Danios keep calm and carry on, zipping around like tiny underwater torpedoes. Their resilience lies in their ability to tolerate a wide range of water parameters, making them perfect for novice aquarists who are still figuring out the whole pH and temperature balancing act. Plus, their low aggression levels mean they won't be picking fights at the fishy dinner table. They're the peaceful party-goers who just want to swim and let swim.

And then there are Guppies, the vibrant peacocks of the aquarium world. These little guys are like the social butterflies at your party, breeding like there's no tomorrow and adding a splash of color to their surroundings. Guppies come in a dizzying array of colors and patterns, each one more dazzling than the last. They're easy to care for, even for the most inexperienced aquarist. Their laid-back attitude and adaptability to various water conditions make them ideal for beginners. Guppies thrive in tanks where the water parameters aren't fluctuating wildly, so a steady hand on the thermostat and regular water changes will keep them happy and healthy. Just be prepared for their prolific breeding habits—they'll multiply faster than you can say "guppy gang."

For caring for these hardy species, it's all about balance. Zebra Danios and Guppies aren't fussy eaters; they'll happily chow down on a variety of foods. A balanced diet of high-quality flakes or pellets, supplemented with the occasional treat of live or frozen food, keeps them in top form. Think of it as offering them a well-rounded menu, ensuring they get all the nutrients they need to stay vibrant. For tank conditions, aim for a stable temperature around 72-78°F and a pH range of 6.5 to 7.5. These parameters mimic their natural habitats, keeping them in their comfort zone and reducing stress.

Now, let's hear from some aquarists who have thrived with these beginner-friendly fish. Take Amy, for example. She started with a simple 10-gallon setup, stocked with a lively group of Guppies. With a bit of patience and regular maintenance, her tank became a kaleidoscope of color, with Guppies darting around like confetti at a parade. And then there's Jake, who opted for a mixed-species tank. He combined Zebra Danios with Guppies, creating a dynamic environment where the two species coexisted peacefully. His secret? Keeping the tank well-planted to provide hiding spots and mitigate any potential squabbles. Each aquarist found success by understanding the unique needs of their fish and creating an environment where they could flourish.

Case Study: The 10-Gallon Wonder

Meet Emily, a newbie aquarist who embarked on her fish keeping adventure with a humble 10-gallon tank. She chose Guppies for their vibrant colors and easy-going nature. With careful attention to water parameters and regular water changes, Emily's tank blossomed into a lively ecosystem. Her Guppies thrived, and she even witnessed the miracle of a new fry joining the family. Emily's story shows that with a bit of dedication and a splash of creativity, even a small tank can become a thriving aquatic paradise.

Peaceful Community Fish: Building a Cohesive Aquatic Family

What if your aquarium was a vibrant little neighborhood where everyone gets along, shares the same pool, and never argues over what's on TV? That's the magic of a well-balanced community tank—a peaceful blend of diverse fish species, each playing their part in a colorful underwater story.

The beauty of a community tank lies in its harmony. Fish of all shapes, sizes, and shades live side by side, creating a dynamic, mesmerizing scene. With the right mix, they move through the water like neighbors waving hello—peaceful, purposeful, and drama-free. It becomes more than a tank; it's a living, breathing work of art that brings calm and curiosity to any room.

But like any friendly neighborhood, it's all about choosing the right residents.

Let's start with a few classic favorites. Neon Tetras are the social butterflies of the aquarium world. People know these sparkling little swimmers for their love of group life and their dazzling, electric colors. Watching a school of them glide through the tank is like seeing a synchronized swim team performing in perfect unison. They bring rhythm and light to the mid-water.

Now look down to the tank floor and you'll spot the Corydoras Catfish, the gentle janitors of your underwater world. These peaceful little bottom-dwellers cruise the substrate, tidying up leftovers like it's their full-time job—and they do it all without causing a stir. Kind-hearted, cute, and hardworking? Yes, please.

Before you start inviting fish to your underwater block party, though, make sure everyone's going to get along. Compatibility isn't just about who's peaceful—it's also about who thrives in the same conditions. Matching fish by water preferences (like temperature, pH, and hardness) helps keep the peace. Think of it as setting the thermostat in your home. You want it comfy for everyone.

Also consider personality and size. A tiny, mellow fish might not enjoy sharing space with a hyper, bossy roommate. It's like planning the seating chart for a dinner party. You want a lively mix, not chaos over the mashed potatoes.

If you're looking for ideas, start simple. A classic and foolproof setup is Neon Tetras + Corydoras. It's an easy, beautiful combo that covers both mid water and bottom zones, creating balance and motion without conflict.

Feeling bold? Try a mixed schooling setup. Think Harlequin Rasboras mingling with Neon Tetras. When done right, you'll have a mesmerizing dance of color and motion that'll have your guests stopping to watch. Just be sure they like the same water conditions and that you give them enough room to breathe and swim.

In the end, building a peaceful aquatic family takes a little planning, a pinch of creativity, and a good helping of patience. But when it all comes together? You've got yourself a miniature world where every fish has its place and every glance into the tank feels like a moment of quiet joy.

Understanding Fish Behavior: Signs of Stress and Aggression

Visualize your fish as the aquatic equivalent of a canary in a coal mine, silently (and sometimes not so silently) signaling when something's amiss. Recognizing these signals is crucial to ensuring your fishy friends remain healthy and happy. One of the most telling signs of stress is rapid gill movement. If your fish are huffing and puffing like they're running an underwater marathon, it's time to investigate. Rapid gill movement often suggests poor water quality, which means it's time for you to roll up your sleeves and check those water parameters. Another red flag is an erratic swimming pattern. Fish zooming around like they've had a bit too much fishy caffeine might try to escape an uncomfortable environment or problematic tank mates. Identifying these behaviors early can make all the difference between a thriving tank and a stressed-out aquarium.

But what causes this aquatic angst? Overcrowding is a primary culprit. Imagine being crammed into a tiny elevator with a dozen strangers—it's not exactly a recipe for Zen. Fish need their space, and too many fins in the tank can lead to territorial disputes. Poor water quality is another stressor. High ammonia or nitrite levels can turn your tank into a toxic wasteland, leading to stress and even aggression. Tank decor, or the lack thereof, also plays a role. Without enough hiding spots, fish can become anxious, feeling exposed. This vulnerability can lead to skirmishes, as fish jostle for the limited real estate of safe zones.

Now, how do you calm these aquatic nerves? Start by increasing hiding spots with plants and decorations. Think of it as building a fishy Fort Knox, where everyone has a private nook to retreat to. Adding caves, rock formations, or dense plantings can reduce stress, offering fish a place to escape from any overzealous tank mates. Adjusting the tank layout can also help ease territorial conflicts. Rearrange decorations and plants to break up sightlines and create distinct territories within the tank. This rearrangement can disrupt existing hierarchies and reduce aggression, much like giving your fish a fresh start in a new neighborhood.

To illustrate the power of these interventions, let's look at a real-life example. Meet the case of Bob, an aquarist who faced a stress-induced frenzy in his tank. Bob noticed his fish were more jittery than a cat on a hot tin roof, with rapid gill movements and frantic darting about. He quickly realized that he had overcrowded his tank, stressing his fish because of the lack of hiding places. By adding a few more plants and rearranging the tank decor, Bob provided much-needed cover and territory for his fish. The transformation was remarkable. The fish calmed down, the aggression dissipated, and Bob's tank became a tranquil oasis once more.

Another success story comes from Linda, who dealt with a similar issue. Her fish were engaged in territorial disputes, causing chaos in her carefully curated community tank. By increasing the number of hiding spots and adjusting the layout, Linda calmed the waters. The fish established their territories, and the tank became peaceful again. Linda's experience shows that sometimes a little habitat enrichment can go a long way in reducing stress and fostering peaceful coexistence.

"How to Tell If Your Fish Are Stressed"

IS YOUR FISH STRESSED?

Watch for signs like rapid gill movement, hiding, or erratic swimming. A few small changes can make a big difference in your fish's comfort and health.

Fish Compatibility: Creating a Balanced Bio load

Imagine your fish are the canaries in your underwater coal mine—silent messengers swimming around, giving off clues when something's not quite right. The trick is knowing what to look for before things go sideways.

Let's start with one of the biggest red flags: rapid gill movement. If your fish look like they're huffing and puffing after an invisible workout, it usually means something is off in the water. Poor water quality is often the culprit, and it's your cue to grab that test kit and play aquatic detective.

Another common clue? Erratic swimming. If your fish are darting around like they've just had a triple espresso, they may try to escape poor conditions—or each other. These behaviors can be early warning signs of stress, bullying, or plain discomfort.

What causes all this fishy tension? Often, it's overcrowding—too many bodies in too small a space. Picture being packed into an elevator with twelve strangers and no air conditioning. That's how your fish feel when things are too tight.

Poor water quality is another mood-killer. High ammonia or nitrite levels can turn your peaceful tank into a toxic soup. And then there's decor drama. Without enough hiding spots or visual barriers, fish may feel exposed and stressed, leading to territorial squabbles.

So how do you bring back the calm?

Start by adding more hiding places. Think of them as cozy fish apartments. Plants, caves, driftwood, even well-placed decoration can help shy or bullied fish feel secure.

Next, rearrange your tank layout. Changing up the furniture breaks established territories and forces aggressive fish to hit the reset button on their turf wars. It's like moving everyone into a new neighborhood where they've got to learn to get along all over again.

Real Story: Bob's Fishy FrenzyBob noticed his peaceful tank had turned into a battleground. Fish were chasing each other, fins were getting nipped, and everyone looked miserable. He realized the tank was overstocked and lacked adequate hiding places. After adding plants and reorganizing the space, harmony returned. The fish relaxed. The drama disappeared.

Another Win: Linda's Layout FixLinda's community tank had a couple of hotheads stirring the waters. With a little rearranging and some well-placed decor, she gave every fish its own nook. The result? Her tank went from battleground to stable in just a few days.

By tuning into your fish" behavior, you'll get early alerts when something" off. A little observation, a few simple changes, and a sprinkle of patience can restore peace and keep your finned friends healthy, happy, and swimming strongly.

Introducing New Fish: Quarantine and Acclimation Processes

Think of your aquarium as a bustling little city. Your fish are the residents, the plants are the greenery, and your filtration system? That's the hardworking sanitation crew keeping everything clean behind the scenes. But just like any city, if too many folks move in too fast, things can get really messy, real quick.

That's where bioload comes in.

Bioolad is the fancy term for how much waste your fish (and other tank buddies) produce—and how much your system can handle. Every uneaten flake, every little poof of fish poop, every puff of algae—it all adds to the workload. If your filter is the janitor, too many fish means it's working overtime with no coffee breaks.

So, how do you keep your tank from turning into an overstuffed apartment complex?

Start with the golden rule: one inch of fish per gallon of water. It's a simple guideline, but not foolproof. A skinny little neon tetra and a bulky goldfish might both measure three inches—but one leaves behind a lot more mess than the other. Always consider the type of fish, not just the size.

Now let's talk about compatibility. This isn't just about personality, it's about jobs and roles. You want a community where everyone contributes fairly. That means mixing mid-swimmers with bottom dwellers, cleanup crews with grazers, and peaceful personalities with other calm companions.

Pro Tip: Choose fish with complementary behaviors. For example, Otocinclus catfish help with algae control, Corydoras clean the substrate, and schooling fish like rasboras bring movement and beauty to the upper levels. Everyone works together like a little underwater dream team.

Tank size plays a big role too. A 10-gallon tank isn't a mansion—it's more of a cozy studio apartment. You wouldn't put a St. Bernard in there, right? Same goes for fish. Always research the adult size and behavior before bringing home a new resident.

Troubleshooting Aggression: Solutions for a Peaceful Tank

Ah, aggression in a fish tank—the aquatic equivalent of a bar brawl breaking out in your living room. Not quite what you pictured when you dreamed of a peaceful, bubbling oasis, right?

The good news? Even the feistiest fish can learn to get along when the environment is just right. First, let's get to know the usual troublemakers behind these underwater squabbles.

Territorial behavior is often the principal cause. Fish, like people, love their space. When another fish wanders into their claimed a corner of the tank, it's like waving a red flag at a bull. Then you've got mating behavior—some fish get a little... let's say, intense... when they're in the mood, but the tank's too crowded for comfort. And don't forget species incompatibility. Some fish are simply incompatible and cannot share a tank, regardless of your attempts at mediation.

So, how do you turn your battlefield back into a peaceful paradise?

1. **Rearrange the Tank**

One of the easiest fixes is simply mixing up the furniture. Reorganizing your plants, rocks, and decor can "reset" territorial claims and create new zones. Think of it as shaking up the seating chart at a tense family dinner.

1. **Add More Hiding Spots**

All fish need a private nook, somewhere they can chill out, hide from bullies, or nap without being pestered. Dense plantings, driftwood, and little caves give your fish those cozy hideouts where they can relax and feel safe.

1. **Feed Thoughtfully**

Fish get hangry too. A poor feeding routine can lead to aggressive behavior during mealtimes. Keep your tank calm by feeding on a schedule and offering a variety of food types that satisfy different dietary needs. A happy, full of fish is far less likely to go looking for trouble.

Real-World Fixes

Case 1: The Time-Out Tank. One aquarist had a rogue fish terrorizing the tank. A simple divider gave everyone a break. After a few days apart, the aggressor calmed down, and the tank settled into a more peaceful rhythm. Like a timeout for fish with surprisingly excellent results.

Case 2: Plant Therapy, another keeper, added more plants and shuffled the decor. Suddenly, the tension eased. Fish stopped chasing each other, and the tank transformed into a calm, beautiful space—like a mini aquatic forest spa retreat.

Aggression isn't always about bad fish—it's often about bad layout, bad timing, or unmet needs. With a little observation, a touch of strategy, and a dose of patience, you can restore balance. And remember, fishkeeping is a living art. If things go wrong, it's not a failure, it's a chance to learn, grow, and fine-tune your watery world.

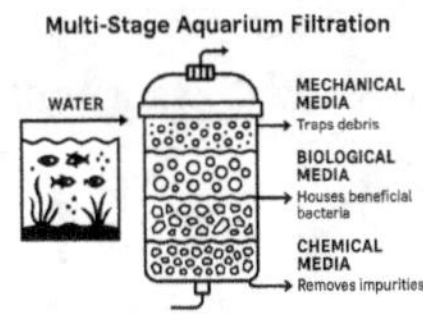

A diagram of a multi-stage aquarium filtration

AI-generated content may be incorrect.

Filter Media Choices: Customizing for Your Aquarium its Needs

Choosing the right filter media for your aquarium is like selecting the perfect toppings for a pizza. Sure, you could just stick with plain cheese, but where's the fun in that? Just as every pizza aficionado has their own preferences, your tank has specific needs that the right media can satisfy.

High-flow media are perfect for large tanks. They're like turbo-charged engines, pushing water through quickly to keep everything sparkling clean. On the flip side, if you're dealing with delicate species that don't appreciate being swept up in a mini hurricane, **fine media** is your best friend. It gently strains out particles, creating a calm flow your sensitive fish will glide through with ease.

The choice of media directly affects your filtration efficiency. **Dense sponges** are fantastic for trapping fine particles—the lint rollers of the aquarium world. They grab debris that would slip through larger pores, helping keep your water looking sharp. Then there's **bio-media**, the bacterial condo complex. With its high surface area, it gives beneficial bacteria plenty of space to move in and do their job—breaking down harmful waste and supporting a stable, healthy tank.

Now here's where things get fun: **customizing your media**. Think of it like building a playlist for your tank—each element adds its own vibe. Combining coarse and fine sponges gives you layered filtration, like filtering your coffee twice for that ultra-smooth finish. The coarse layer grabs the big stuff; the fine sponge picks up what's left behind.

Want extra polish? Add **Purigen** or another premium water polisher. These small but mighty media give your tank that glassy, show-off-the-aquascape clarity—like a freshly cleaned window on a sunny day. It's the finishing touch for aquarists who want both beauty and balance.

Let's look at a few real-world setups to bring it home:

- **Busy Aquarist?** Try a low-maintenance combo: bio-media + coarse sponge in a compact canister filter. Minimal fuss, maximum effectiveness.

- **Heavily Stocked Tank?** Go all-in: coarse sponge → bio-balls → activated carbon → polishing layer (like Purigen). It's your dream team for tackling waste like pros on a cleaning crew.

- **Small Peaceful Tank?** A gentle sponge filter with a pinch of bio-media does the trick—easy on fry, shrimp, or bettas.

Finding the *optimal media mix* is a bit like building your signature pizza. It might take a few tries to get the balance just right—but when you hit that sweet spot? It's pure satisfaction.

Chapter 5: The Science of Filtration

Ensuring Crystal–Clear Water with the Right Tools, Techniques, and Troubleshooting Tips

What if your aquarium was a bustling aquatic metropolis? Your fish are the citizens, your plants are the lush city parks, and the filter? That's your sanitation department—quietly working behind the scenes to keep the streets clean and the water fresh.

Filtration is the unsung hero of any tank. Without it, your peaceful underwater world would quickly turn into swampy chaos. Cloudy water, stressed-out fish, and funky smells? That's what happens when filtration isn't up to snuff.

But don't worry, we're going to break it down and make it simple. In this chapter, we'll explore the three types of filtration every aquarist needs to know:

1. Mechanical–the "debris catcher"

2. Biological–the "bacteria brigade"

3. Chemical–the "toxin trapper"

Each one plays a vital role in keeping your tank as clean and comfy as a five-star spa, for fish, anyway.

Mechanical Filtration: Your Tank's Vacuum Cleaner

Mechanical filtration is like the bouncer at the club—its job is to keep the unwanted stuff out. This system physically removes solid gunk from the water, like uneaten food, fish poop, and floating debris. Filter pads and sponges are the MVPs here, trapping the muck before it can cause problems.

But here's the catch: like any good vacuum, your filter needs regular cleaning. Otherwise, it'll clog up faster than your teenager's group chat, and a clogged filter is about as useful as a chocolate teapot.

Biological Filtration: Nature's Cleanup Crew

Now this is where the real magic happens. Biological filtration relies on helpful bacteria—tiny, hardworking microbes that quietly handle the messy stuff. These good bacteria grow on your filter media (like ceramic rings or bio-balls) and convert toxic fish waste (ammonia and nitrite) into much safer nitrate.

Think of them as invisible janitors that never sleep, constantly breaking down waste and keeping your water safe. But they need time to settle in. Don" scrub too hard or rinse them in chlorinated tap water, you'll wipe out your bacteria colony faster than you can say ""tank crash.""Chemical Filtration: The Water's Detox.

Chemical filtration:

Is like your tank" detox program—it helps remove toxins, discoloration, and smells. Activated carbon is the go-to here. It works like a sponge, absorbing all kinds of unwanted substances and keeping the water fresh.

You can also use specialty media like ion exchange resins, which target things like heavy metals or soften your water. These media don" last forever, though—so mark your calendar and replace them regularly to keep them effective.

Putting It All Together

- Many filters combine all three filtration types into one system. For example:

- Canister filters: Powerful, quiet, and tucked out of sight. Great for larger tanks.

- Hang-on-back (HOB) filters: easy to use, customizable, and perfect for beginners.

- Sponge filters: Gentle and great for small tanks, shrimp, or breeding setups.

Each system has its perks, and choosing the right one depends on your tank size, fish load, and how much maintenance you want to do.

Visual Element: Filtration System Diagram

A clean black-and-white sketch that shows water flowing through the three stages—mechanical, biological, chemical—with each labeled clearly.

Maintaining Your Filter: Cleaning and Replacement Schedules

Filters may work behind the scenes, but don't let their quiet nature fool you—they need regular care to keep doing their job. Think of your filter as a loyal friend who takes out your trash every day. But if you never check on them? Eventually, they'll stop showing up.

Proper maintenance isn't just about cleaning—it's about knowing what to clean, when to clean it, and how not to ruin your beneficial bacteria.

Mechanical Media (Sponges, Pads, Floss)

These are the gunk-grabbers. They trap solid waste and leftover food before it breaks down into nastier stuff.

How often?

- Check weekly.

- Rinse every 1–2 weeks in old tank water (never tap!) to avoid killing helpful bacteria.

- Replace when it starts to fall apart or clog consistently.

Biological Media (Ceramic Rings, Bio-Balls)

These are the homes for your beneficial bacteria. Their job is too important to mess with casually.

How often?

- Clean only when necessary, maybe once a month or every other month.

- Use gentle swishing in tank water (never soap or hot water).

- Never replace unless it's crumbling or severely damaged.

Chemical Media (Carbon, Purigen, Resins)

These are your water polishers and detox specialists. Unlike the others, they don't regenerate and will lose effectiveness overtime.

How often?

- Activated carbon: Replace every 3–4 weeks.

- Purigen: Recharge or replace monthly, or when water clarity drops.

- Specialty resins: Follow package instructions—some last longer, some require recharging.

Filter Cleaning Do's & Don'ts
Do:

- Unplug your filter before maintenance (safety first!)

- Use old tank water for rinsing media

- Keep filter parts assembled in the correct order

- Clean impellers and housing every 1–2 months

Don't:

- Use tap water directly on biological media

- Clean all media at once (rotate instead)

- Let your filter run dry after reassembly

- Toss out media unless it's necessary

Real-Life Rhythm: The Monthly Filter Flow
A simple schedule can go a long way:

- Weekly: Check flow, wipe glass, and peek inside the filter

- Biweekly: Rinse mechanical media

- Monthly: Swish biological media, replace or recharge chemical media

- Every 2–3 months: Deep clean the impeller and tubing

Keeping up with this routine helps prevent ammonia spikes, keeps your bacteria colony happy, and ensures your tank water stays clear and breathable for your finned friends.

DIY Filtration Solutions: Creative and Cost-Effective Options

Picture this: you're staring at your aquarium, dreaming of the perfect filter setup that won't cost you an arm and a leg. Enter the world of DIY filtration solutions, where creativity and ingenuity come together to save you some serious cash. Building a custom filtration system is more than just a budget-friendly alternative to commercial filters; it's a chance to tailor your setup to your tank's unique needs. Imagine constructing a filter that fits just right, like a custom-made suit for your aquatic home. Not only do you get to pocket the savings, but you also enjoy the satisfaction of knowing you built something with your own hands—like crafting your very own underwater Batcave.

Creating a DIY filter doesn't require a degree in engineering or a magic wand. You can start with something as simple as a sponge filter. All you need is a sponge, some tubing, and an air pump. The sponge acts as a physical barrier, trapping debris while providing a home for beneficial bacteria. It's like hosting a block party for bacteria, and everyone's invited. To make it, attach the sponge to the bottom of the tubing, connect the air pump, and voilà! You've got yourself a simple yet effective filter that won't break the bank. For those feeling a bit more adventurous, try your hand at a trickle filter using household items like plastic bottles and filter floss. Assemble the bottles into a cascading setup, allowing water to trickle through the media, capturing debris and purifying the water. It's like a DIY waterfall, mesmerizing to watch and functional at the same time.

DIY filtration systems are effective for small tanks and budget-friendly setups. They allow you to customize your filtration based on the bioload and specific needs of your aquarium inhabitants. However, they're not without limitations. DIY solutions might struggle with larger tanks or heavy bio loads, where a more robust system is necessary to keep up with the waste production. It's like expecting a bicycle to tow a trailer—doable, but not ideal. Despite these challenges, many aquarists have successfully implemented DIY filters with impressive results.

Consider the story of an aquarist who built a DIY sump system using a series of plastic containers, PVC pipes, and filter media. By designing the sump to fit snugly under their tank, they could create a highly efficient filtration system that rivaled commercial options. They reported crystal-clear water and lucky fish, all without spending a fortune. Another DIY enthusiast crafted a custom canister filter using a 5-gallon bucket and some clever modifications. The filter successfully maintained a 40-gallon tank, demonstrating the power of DIY ingenuity. These examples showcase the potential of DIY filters to deliver high-quality results without the hefty price tag.

DIY VS. STORE-BOUGHT FILTER

Feature	DIY Filter	Store-Bought Filter
$ Cost	Under $10	$20-$100+
Customization	High	Low-Medium
Filtration typ	Basic	Multi-stage
Setup time	Slower	Plug-and-play
Maintnance	Varies	Consistent
Best For	Small tanks, budget builds	Larger tanks, convenience

Whether you're building your own filter or buying one off the shelf, the best option is the one that matches your tank size, budget, and time for maintenance.

Troubleshooting Filtration Issues: Diagnosing Common Problems

Picture this: you're staring at your aquarium, dreaming up the perfect filter setup—one that works like a charm but doesn't drain your wallet. Welcome to the world of DIY filtration, where a little creativity, a few simple tools, and some budget-friendly brilliance can go a long way.

Building your own filter isn't just about saving money (though it definitely helps)—it's about customizing your system to fit your tank's exact needs. It's like tailoring a suit for your aquatic home. And there's something deeply satisfying about standing back and saying, *"I made that."* Think of it as building your own underwater Batcave—functional, stealthy, and totally cool.

Start Simple: The Classic DIY Sponge Filter

No engineering degree required just a sponge, some airline tubing, and an air pump. The sponge does double duty: trapping debris while giving beneficial bacteria a cozy place to live. It" like hosting a block party for your tank" bio-crew.

To make one:

- Attach the sponge to the bottom of the rigid tubing

- Connect the tubing to an air pump

- Place it in the tank and plug it in and Voila! You've got a functional, affordable, and gentle filter, especially great for fry, shrimp, or nano tanks.

Go Big (ger): DIY Trickle Filter

If you're feeling more adventurous, try a DIY trickle filter using everyday items like plastic water bottles, filter floss, and gravity. Stack the bottles into a vertical tower, punch drainage holes, and let water cascade through layers of media. It" like creating a mini waterfall—and yes, it's as satisfying to build as it is to watch.

These systems offer a surprising level of biological and mechanical filtration for something built with household items.

Real-World DIY Wins

DIY filters really shine in small tanks, breeding setups, or low-budget builds, where flexibility and simplicity matter most. While they're not ideal for heavy bioloads or large aquariums (it's like asking a bike to tow a trailer, doable but not optimal), they can still deliver impressive results.

Take the aquarist who built a DIY sump system from plastic containers, PVC pipe, and scavenged filter media. It tucked neatly under the stand and performed like a champ, keeping water crystal-clear, without the price tag of a commercial sump.

Another keeper made a DIY canister filter from a 5-gallon bucket, sealed lids, and clever plumbing. It ran a 40-gallon tank reliably, proving that with some ingenuity, duct tape (figuratively), and patience, you can build a filter system that holds its own.

DIY filtration isn't just about saving money, it's about understanding your tank, adapting to its needs, and having a little fun along the way. Whether you're working with shrimp or showstoppers, there's a certain pride in saying, "I filtered that myself."

Enhancing Filtration Efficiency: Tips and Techniques

You've got your filter up and running, but just like squeezing the last bit of toothpaste out of the tube, there's always a little more you can do to optimize performance. Adjusting flow rates is a key step. It's like tuning a guitar, too fast, and your fish might feel like they're in a washing machine; too slow, and debris piles up like dirty laundry. Finding that sweet spot ensures your water turnover is just right, creating a stable environment for your aquatic buddies. And don't overlook the importance of filter positioning. It's all about achieving even circulation, much like trying to spread peanut butter evenly on toast. Place your filter in a spot where it can distribute water effectively, avoiding dead zones where debris and waste can accumulate.

If you want to take things up a notch, consider adding some complementary equipment to your setup. UV sterilizers are fantastic for keeping algae in check. Think of them as the bouncers of your tank, keeping unwanted guests like algae spores at bay. They work by zapping these pesky invaders with ultraviolet light, preventing them from turning your tank into a green, swampy mess. And let's not forget surface skimmers, which work wonders in removing debris from the water's surface. They're like your tank's personal cleaning crew, ensuring the top layer remains pristine and free from floating particles. By incorporating these tools, you can enhance water quality and provide a healthier environment for your fish.

To maintain peak efficiency, regular calibration of flow rates and settings is a must. It's like tuning up your car for a road trip—ensuring everything runs smoothly and efficiently. Keep an eye out for obstructions in the intake and output areas, as these can hinder performance. Think of it as checking your vacuum cleaner for clogs—essential for keeping everything running smoothly. Regular maintenance helps prevent these issues, ensuring your filter operates at its best.

Now, let's peek into the world of advanced filtration setups. Imagine a multi-tiered filtration system working in harmony with a complex aquascape. These setups are like a symphony of efficiency, with each stage handling a different aspect of filtration. The result? Crystal-clear water that showcases every detail of your underwater masterpiece. Then there's the concept of incorporating refugiums for nutrient export. It's like having a secret garden tucked away in your tank, where plants and macroalgae absorb excess nutrients, reducing the risk of nuisance algae. These advanced systems show the potential of filtration to transform your tank into a thriving ecosystem.

As we wrap up this chapter on filtration, remember that optimizing your filtration system is about more than just keeping your water clear. It's about creating a stable and healthy environment where your fish can thrive. With the right strategies and tools, you can enhance your filtration efficiency, ensuring your tank remains a vibrant and inviting habitat. Now, get ready to explore the fascinating dynamics of fish behavior and compatibility in the next chapter, where we'll dive into the world of finned friendships and harmonious communities.

Chapter 6: Mastering Aquarium Maintenance: Routine Care for Thriving Tanks

• • • • • • • • • •

TimeSaving Tips, Cleaning Routines, and Seasonal Adjustments for a Low-Stress, High-Reward Hobby

Now what if your aquarium is a tiny, bustling metropolis, where fish are the citizens, plants are the parks, and you're the mayor responsible for keeping everything in tip-top shape? And like any good mayor, you've got to ensure your city doesn't fall into chaos with a bit of regular maintenance. Without it, your gorgeous aquatic world could become like a city during a garbage strike, messy, smelly, and downright unlivable. But don't worry, with a little elbow grease and a sprinkle of routine, you'll have your underwater utopia thriving in no time. Let's jump into the world of weekly maintenance, where consistency and a good checklist are your best friends.

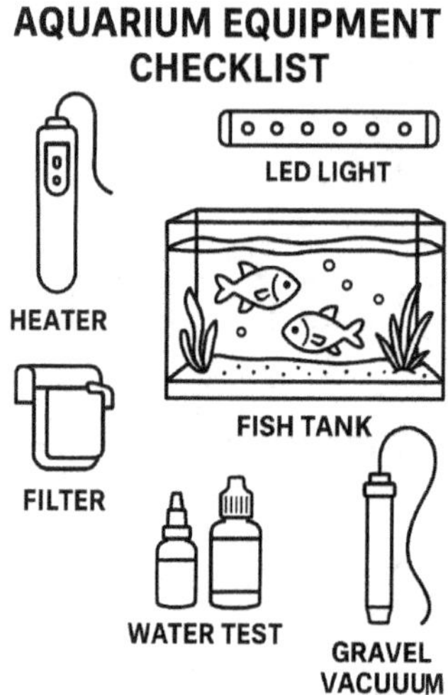

*From setup to cleaning, these basic tools
make aquarium care easy, affordable,
and beginner-friendly.*

Weekly Maintenance Routines: The Key to a Healthy Aquarium

First up, let's talk about checking water parameters. Think of it as taking the pulse of your aquarium. You wouldn't want your fish swimming in a chemical soup, so testing for ammonia, nitrite, and nitrate levels is crucial. A simple test kit is your stethoscope, providing you with all the vital signs you need. Adjusting these parameters is like tweaking the thermostat at home, too hot or too cold, and the residents get cranky. Monitor the pH too, because just like you wouldn't want to drink overly acidic or basic water, neither do your fish. Regular checks prevent nasty surprises and keep your fish happily swimming along.

Next, inspect your equipment like a detective on the case. Filters, heaters, and lights are your trusty sidekicks, but even the best sidekicks need a little TLC. Ensure that gunk hasn't clogged your filter; a clogged filter is as useful as a chocolate teapot. Check that your heater is keeping things toasty and your lights are still shining bright. A quick inspection can save you from a world of trouble down the line. It's like checking your car's oil, ignore it and you could end up stranded on the side of the road, or in this case, with a tank full of unhappy fish.,

Consistency is key for maintenance, much like brushing your teeth or doing your homework. Regular care prevents long-term issues, reducing stress on your fish and preventing waste buildup. A stable environment is like a comfy pair of slippers for your fish, keeping them relaxed and happy. Neglecting maintenance is like skipping all your dentist appointments for a year. Sure, you might get away with it for a while, but eventually, things will come crashing down.

Incorporating maintenance into your daily life doesn't have to be a chore. Set reminders on your phone or stick a calendar on your fridge. Create a checklist that outlines all the tasks you need to accomplish. It's like having a personal trainer for your aquarium, keeping you on track and motivated. Break it into manageable chunks so it doesn't feel overwhelming. And remember, a little maintenance each week keeps your fish from staging a mutiny.

Let's look at a successful maintenance schedule from an experienced aquarist. Every Sunday, they spend just 30 minutes on their tank, ticking off tasks from their checklist. First, they test water parameters, adjusting as needed. Then, they inspect the equipment, ensuring everything is in working order. Next, they perform a partial water change, removing about 20% of the old water and replacing it with fresh, conditioned water. Finally, they clean the tank glass and trim any overgrown plants. This routine keeps their aquarium thriving, with minimal stress and maximum enjoyment.

For those with busy lifestyles, time-efficient techniques are a must. Consider multitasking test water while your morning coffee brews, or inspect equipment during TV commercials. Break tasks into smaller segments throughout the week, so maintenance doesn't feel like a marathon. And remember, the goal is to enjoy your aquarium, not let it become a burden. With a little planning and a touch of humor, your weekly maintenance routine can be a breeze, keeping your aquatic city a bustling, beautiful place for all its residents.

Spotting and Treating Fish Illnesses: Early Detection and Action

Assume you're a fish whisperer, tuning into the subtle signals your aquatic pals send when they're feeling in the weather. It's like being Dr. Doolittle, but instead of chatting with horses, you're deciphering the body language of your fishy friends. Spotting illness early is the key to keeping your tank a harmonious haven. Keep an eye out for changes in color or behavior. Maybe your vibrant neon tetra looks dull, or your normally energetic guppy is hiding out more than usual. These shifts are like your fish waving a little white flag, asking for help.

Visible lesions or fin damage are also red flags. They're like the aquarium version of a stubbed toe, obviously and in need of attention. Early detection is crucial because it gives you a fighting chance to nip problems in the bud before they spiral into full-blown fishy dramas. Quarantine procedures are your first line of defense. They're like the quarantine section in the airport, ensuring that any new fish or plants don't bring unwanted hitchhikers into your tank. Regular observation of behavioral changes is equally important. Set aside a few minutes each day to just watch your fish. It's like a mini meditation session that not only relaxes you but also lets you catch any odd behavior before it becomes a big issue.

Once you've spotted something amiss, it's time to channel your inner fish doctor and get to work. Treating various fish illnesses involves a few different approaches. For internal parasites, medicated food is your best bet. It's like giving your fish a dose of antibiotics hidden inside a delicious treat. Just be sure to follow the instructions carefully, as overdosing can cause more harm than good. For external infections, topical treatments are the way to go. These are like the aquarium equivalent of antiseptic cream, dealing with things like fungal infections or bacterial sores. Apply them carefully and ensure your fish get some downtime in a hospital tank to recover away from the hustle and bustle of their usual environment.

Case studies of successful treatment interventions can provide some inspiration. Take the story of a dedicated aquarist who noticed one of their angelfish developing suspicious white spots. With a quick diagnosis of ich, they implemented a course of medicated food and raised the tank temperature slightly to speed up the parasites' life cycle. Within a week, the angelfish was back to its usual elegant self, and the rest of the tank remained unaffected thanks to swift quarantine measures. Another tale involves a goldfish with visible fin rot. The owner promptly isolated it and applied a topical antibacterial treatment. With regular water changes and a bit of TLC, the goldfish made a full recovery, its fins regrowing beautifully.

We cannot overstate the importance of quarantine. It's the aquarium equivalent of washing your hands before eating—simple, effective, and crucial for preventing outbreaks. By keeping a close eye on recent additions in a separate tank, you can catch potential issues before they infect your entire community. It's like having a VIP lounge for your fish, ensuring they're in tip-top shape before joining the main event. In the realm of fishkeeping, early detection and action are your best allies. If you pay attention and take care of your fish, they will stay healthy and your tank will be clean.

Managing Algae Growth: Prevention and Control Strategies

Picture this: you wake up one morning and your beautiful aquarium has turned into a scene from a swamp horror movie. Algae have taken over like an uninvited guest, lounging on your rocks and turning your crystal-clear water into a green soup. But fear not, for understanding why algae blooms occur is your first step to reclaiming your tank. Algae thrive on excess nutrients, which often sneak in through overfeeding. Those extra food flakes you toss in for your fish. They're like a buffet for algae, inviting them to settle in and stay a while. Combine that with an imbalance in light exposure—too much light, and algae think they've found paradise. It's like leaving your porch light on and wondering why bugs won't leave you alone.

So, how do you show algae to the door? Regular water changes are your best friend. By swapping out 10-15% of the water each week, you reduce nutrient levels and keep algae from setting up shop. It's a bit like sweeping crumbs off the kitchen floor before ants find them. Adjusting light duration and intensity is another effective strategy. Keep lighting to about 8-10 hours a day and avoid placing your tank in direct sunlight unless you want an algae jungle. A timer can help you manage this, turning lights on and off automatically so you don't have to worry about it. Think of it as setting up a curfew for your tank—lights out, algae.

Now, what if algae has already made themselves at home? It's time to get started. Manual removal using algae scrapers is your go-to. It's like giving your tank a good scrub, getting rid of that green fuzz clinging to surfaces. For stubborn patches, a little elbow grease goes a long way. But why do all the work yourself? Introducing algae-eating fish or invertebrates can be a significant change. Consider adding a Siamese algae eater or some snails to your community. These critters munch away at algae, keeping it in check while adding a bit of life to your tank. It's like hiring a cleaning crew that also entertains.

There are plenty of aquarists who have battled algae and come out victorious. Take the story of one determined hobbyist who faced a persistent green water issue. By reducing feeding, performing regular water changes, and adding a few algae-eating shrimp, they restored their tank's clarity. Another aquarist struggled with brown algae on their plants. After adjusting the light cycle and introducing a handful of Otocinclus catfish, they achieved a balanced ecosystem, with algae under control and plants flourishing. These examples show that with patience and a few strategic moves, you can keep your aquarium looking stunning.

Managing algae growth is all about balance nutrition, light, and the right tank residents. By understanding the causes and implementing these strategies, you can maintain a healthy, vibrant aquarium that's free from the clutches of algae.

Cleaning Techniques: Gravel Vacuuming and Glass Scraping

Think of gravel vacuuming as your tank's version of spring cleaning. It might not sound thrilling, but it's an absolute must keep your underwater kingdom free of the muck and grime that can build up. Now, picture a siphon, a simple tool that's about as miraculous as a magic wand for debris removal. Start by submerging the siphon in the tank to fill it with water, then create a flow using gravity by lowering the other end into a bucket. It's like siphoning gas, minus the illegal part. Move the siphon over the gravel in a gentle, circular motion. This helps suck up all that detritus without disturbing the gravel too much. For those pesky corners and tight spots, tilt the siphon slightly or use a smaller attachment to reach every nook and cranny. It's like vacuuming under the couch, where dust bunnies like to hide.

Now, onto glass scraping. There's nothing worse than looking at your fish through a layer of algae, like trying to watch TV through a fogged-up window. Magnetic scrapers are your best friend here. These handy tools allow you to clean the inside of the tank while keeping your hands dry. Just attach one side of the magnet to the outside of the glass and the other to the inside, then move them around in a slow, steady motion. It's like wiping down a whiteboard, but with a lot more satisfaction involved. To prevent scratches, avoid using anything abrasive. If you notice a stubborn spot, resist the urge to get aggressive. Instead, a soft sponge or algae pad should do the trick. Remember, gentle is the name of the game.

Taking care of your cleaning tools is just as important as the cleaning itself. After each use, rinse your siphon and scraper thoroughly with clean water to remove any residue. Dry them off before storing to prevent mold or mildew from setting in. Check your tools regularly for signs of wear and tear. A cracked siphon tube or worn-out scraper pad won't do you any favors in the long run. Replace parts as needed to keep your cleaning routine running smoothly. It's like maintaining your car—regular checks and timely replacements keep everything in tip-top shape.

For those looking to streamline their cleaning routine, efficiency is key. Combine tasks where possible. While you're vacuuming the gravel, inspect your plants for dead leaves and trim as needed. Use multi-functional tools, such as a siphon with a built-in scraper or a sponge with a scrubbing pad, to tackle multiple tasks without switching gear. This way, you can get more done in less time, leaving you with more moments to sit back and enjoy your tank's beauty.

Visual Element: Cleaning Checklist

Weekly Tasks

1. **Check Water Levels** Top off evaporated water with treated tap water.

2. **Test Water Parameters** Check ammonia, nitrite, nitrate, pH, and temperature.

3. **Clean Aquarium Glass** Use an algae scraper or sponge to remove buildup.

4. **Gravel Vacuuming** Siphon debris from the substrate during your water change.

5. **Partial Water Change (20-30%)**Remove and replace with clean, treated water.

6. **Rinse Filter Media (In Tank Water)**Gently rinse mechanical media (sponges or pads) in used tank water to avoid killing beneficial bacteria.

Monthly Tasks

1. **Deep Clean Decorations** Gently scrub décor with aquarium-safe tools if needed.

2. **Check Filter Functionality** Inspect all filter parts and ensure proper water flow.

3. **Replace Chemical Media (If Needed)**Swap out carbon or other chemical media according to manufacturer recommendations.

4. **Inspect Equipment** Check heaters, lights, air pumps, and other equipment for proper operation.

5. **Clean Aquarium Lid and Light** Wipe down dust and water spots to maintain brightness.

Enjoy Your Sparkling Aquarium!

Take a step back, admire your work, and enjoy watching your healthy, happy fish thrive.

Seasonal Maintenance: Adjusting Care Throughout the Year

As the seasons change, so too must your approach to aquarium maintenance. It" like swapping out your wardrobe; just as you wouldn" wear a parka in July, your fish tank has different needs throughout the year. Temperature fluctuations are the most obvious seasonal change, and they can have significant effects on your aquatic buddies. In summer, rising room temperatures can turn your aquarium into a balmy sauna, which might be great for a tropical vacation but not so much for your fish. To cool things down, consider using a fan to increase evaporation or investing in an aquarium chiller for those particularly sweltering days. On the flip side, winter brings the chill, and you will need to ensure your heater is up to the task. A reliable heater keeps the water cozy, preventing your tank from turning into an ice palace.

Lighting also demands attention as the days lengthen and shorten. During summer, your tank might receive extra natural light, which can be as much a blessing as a curse. While it might enhance plant growth, it can also lead to dreaded algae blooms if left unchecked. Consider adjusting your artificial lighting duration to balance the increase in natural light. In winter, when daylight is scarce, you might need to extend artificial lighting to compensate. It" all about finding that sweet spot where your plants thrive without going into algae overdrive.

Monitoring your fish" behavior during seasonal transitions is crucial. Fish are surprisingly perceptive to environmental changes, even if they don" have a calendar to tell them it's time for spring cleaning. Keep an eye out for signs of stress, such as erratic swimming or a sudden disinterest in food. These behaviors can show discomfort because of temperature changes or lighting variations. Adjust the feeding schedules. It" like how we suddenly crave soup instead of ice cream when winter hits. Being vigilant and responsive can prevent minor issues from snowballing into major problems.

Successful seasonal maintenance is all about planning. A seasonal checklist can be your best friend, ensuring you don't overlook important tasks amidst the hustle and bustle of life. In the summer, focus on maintaining optimal water temperatures and adjusting lighting. In the winter, prioritize heating and check for any drafts that might affect your tank's temperature. A little foresight goes a long way in keeping your aquarium stable and your fish happy.

Consider the case of an aquarist who faced a warm summer and noticed their fish displaying signs of heat stress. By implementing a simple fan setup and reducing light duration, they stabilized the environment, preventing any lasting effects on their aquatic community. Conversely, another enthusiast found their tank's temperature dropping during a cold snap. By adding an extra heater and insulating the back of the tank, they maintained a comfortable habitat for their finned friends. These examples show that with a pinch of preparation and a dash of adaptability, you can keep your aquarium thriving no matter the season.

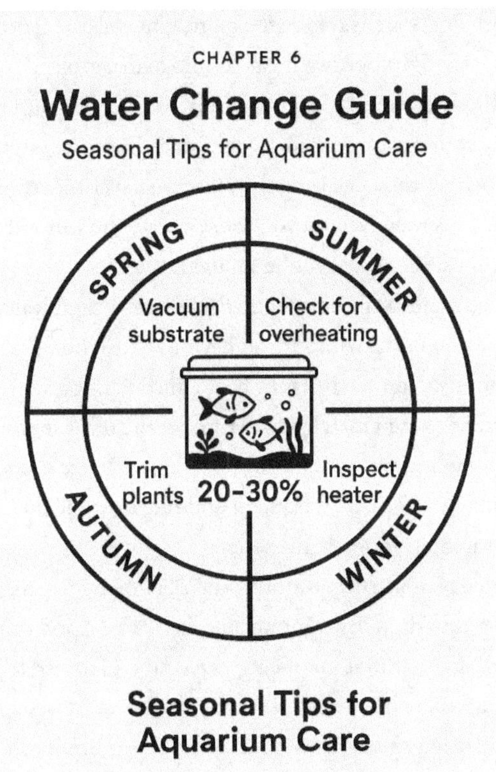

**Seasonal Tips for
Aquarium Care**

*Adjust your maintenance with the seasons: watch the
heater in winter, trim plants in fall, and always
change 20–30% for a happy, stable tank*

Overcoming Maintenance Obstacles: Time Management Tips

Navigating the world of aquarium maintenance can sometimes feel like trying to juggle flaming torches while riding a unicycle. Life gets busy, and before you know it, your tank is looking less like an underwater paradise and more like a science project gone wrong. One of the most common hurdles is a packed schedule that leaves little room for tank care. It's easy to let tasks slip through the cracks when your calendar is fuller than a clown car. Then there's motivation. Some days, the thought of tackling algae or testing water can seem as appealing as cleaning out the garage. The sheer number of tasks can be overwhelming, making it tempting to quit.

But don't despair! There are ways to streamline your maintenance routine and keep things running smoothly. Start by breaking tasks into manageable steps. It's like chopping up a massive to-do list into bite-sized pieces. Instead of spending hours at once, dedicate small chunks of time each day or week to specific tasks. Prioritize essential jobs like water changes and equipment checks, ensuring the most crucial elements of your tank get the attention they need. This way, even on your busiest day, you can still squeeze in a quick check or change without feeling like you're scaling Everest.

Technology can be a lifesaver. Automatic feeders are a significant change, ensuring your fish get their meals on time without you having to rush home from work. It's like a personal chef for your fish, minus the fancy hat. Timed lighting systems can also reduce your workload. By setting your tank's lights to turn on and off at specific times, you maintain a consistent day-night cycle without lifting a finger. These gadgets transform your aquarium into a semi-autonomous ecosystem and free up your time for more pressing matters, like binge-watching your favorite series.

Let's dive into some real-life success stories. Take Sarah, who juggles a full-time job, a family, and a bustling aquarium. By using an automatic feeder and programmable lights, she kept her fish thriving without sacrificing her sanity. Her secret? Setting reminders on her phone for the weekly deep-clean, ensuring she never misses a beat. Then there's Mike, a college student who turned his dorm room aquarium into a low-maintenance masterpiece. By prioritizing regular water changes and using a gravel vacuum with a built-in siphon, he keeps his tank sparkling with minimal effort. His advice? "Find what works for you and stick with it."

Incorporating these strategies into your routine can transform aquarium care from a daunting chore into a manageable part of your weekly schedule. By breaking tasks into smaller steps, using technology, and prioritizing what's important, you'll find more time to enjoy watching your underwater community flourish. Your fish will thank you with their vibrant colors and lively antics, turning what was once a dreaded task into a source of relaxation and enjoyment. And with Chapter 7 just around the corner, we'll explore how engaging the next generation in this hobby can create a lifelong love for aquariums, passing on the torch to future aquarists.

Chapter 7: Engaging the Next Generation: Educating Young Aquarists

Fun Projects, Hands-On Learning, and Family-Friendly Ideas to Spark Lifelong Aquarium Curiosity in Kids

Here's what it might look like: you're a kid again, peering into a glass box full of water, eyes wide with wonder. Inside, fish zip around like tiny, colorful rockets, and plants sway gently like they're grooving to some underwater beat. This isn't just a tank; it's an entire universe waiting to be explored. As you stand there, captivated, you realize this aquarium is more than just a pretty sight. It's a classroom, a science lab, and a playground all rolled into one. Welcome to the world of teaching kids about aquariums, where science meets art and learning is as fun as a splashy cannonball into a pool.

Simplifying Complex Concepts: Teaching Water Chemistry to Kids

Water chemistry might sound like what makes you doze off faster than a lullaby. But with a little creativity, we can turn this complex subject into something as sweet and simple as a glass of lemonade. Imagine pH as the sweetness scale of your lemonade: too sour, and you're puckering up; too sweet, and it's a sugar rush. Fish, like lemonade enthusiasts, prefer their water just right in a Goldilocks zone of pH perfection.

Then there's the nitrogen cycle, which, if you're not careful, can sound about as exciting as watching paint dry. But fear not! Picture it as a cartoon superhero saga, with ammonia as the villain, nitrites as the sidekicks, and nitrates as the unsung heroes. Ammonia wreaks havoc until nitrites step in to save the day, transforming into nitrates and keeping the peace. With cartoon illustrations, this cycle of transformation becomes a dynamic tale of adventure, making chemistry as thrilling as a superhero showdown.

To reinforce these key concepts, nothing beats hands-on activities. Arm your young scientists with pH testing kits and let them play the role of mad scientists, experimenting with water samples like they're concocting potions in a wizard's lab. Games that match fish species to their ideal water conditions turn learning into a playful quest, where each correct match is a victory dance for knowledge. It's all about making science so engaging that even the most reluctant learner can't resist joining in.

For educators and parents, having the right tools is a significant change. Imagine having printable worksheets with fun quizzes that transform learning into a friendly competition, where each correct answer is a step closer to becoming an aquarium ace. Pair these with access to kid-friendly educational videos that bring abstract ideas to life through vibrant visuals and engaging narratives. These resources are like a treasure trove, arming adults with everything they need to transform learning into a captivating journey.

And let's not forget the power of visuals. Color-coded charts for pH levels turn chemistry into a vibrant spectrum of possibilities, where each color represents a different level of acidity or alkalinity. Diagrams of the nitrogen cycle, complete with fish characters embarking on their chemical adventures, make abstract concepts tangible. These visuals are the bridge between complexity and clarity, making chemistry not just understandable but downright delightful. With these tools and strategies, young aquarists can dive into the wonders of water chemistry with excitement, sparking curiosity and setting the stage for a lifelong love of learning.

Interactive Element: DIY pH Testing Kit Experiment

Did you know that water in your fish tank can be too acidic or too basic for your fish and plants? Let's learn about pH by doing a fun science experiment right at home!

What You'll Need:

    1. A pH test kit (strips or drops work great!)

    2. A notebook and pencil to record your results

3. Household liquids such as

- Tap water

- Lemon juice

- Baking soda mixed with water

- Vinegar

- Soda

- Any other safe liquids you have at home

What to Do:

Make a Prediction: Before testing, write down what you think the pH will be for each liquid.Will it be **high** (basic), **low** (acidic), or **neutral**?

Test Each Liquid: Use your **pH test kit** to check each one.Watch the color change and **match it to the chart** to find the number.

Record Your Results: Write the name of the liquid and its pH number.

Compare and Discuss:
- Which liquids were **more acidic** (lower pH)?

- Which were **more basic** (higher pH)?

- Which were **close to neutral** (around 7)?

Why This Matters in Aquariums:
- Fish and plants need the right pH to stay healthy.

- If the water is **too acidic** or **too basic**, it can **stress or harm** them.

- Most freshwater fish like a pH of **6.5 to 7.5**—right in the middle!

Think Like a Scientist:
- How can this experiment help you take better care of your fish tank? Talk about your ideas with a parent, teacher, or friend!

Interactive Learning: Hands-On Aquarium Projects for Children

Picture this: a group of kids gathered around a table, each armed with a tiny glass jar and a heap of enthusiasm. Today, they're not just kids; they're budding aquarists on a mission to create their own mini-aquascapes. These little ecosystems in glass jars are more than just a fun project—they're a gateway to understanding balance and creativity in nature. With a handful of gravel, a sprig of aquatic plant, and a splash of water, these young creators bring to life a tiny world that's as engaging to build as it is to admire. It's a project that encourages active participation, where each choice be it the placement of a pebble or the angle of a leaf—turns into a delightful learning moment.

Now, let's talk about another exciting project: building a terrarium with aquatic plants. This is where land meets water in a harmonious blend of greenery and serenity. Kids can transform a simple container into a lush landscape, complete with stones, moss, and water-loving plants. Imagine them carefully arranging layers of soil and sand, each level a foundation for the next, until they've constructed a living work of art. It's an activity that teaches patience and planning, with the reward of watching their terrarium flourish day by day.

To guide young aquarists through these projects, clear and accessible instructions are key. Setting up a small betta bowl, for instance, starts with selecting the right bowl—a wide, shallow one offers more surface area for air exchange. Add a layer of smooth gravel, a few hardy plants, and, of course, a betta fish with personality to spare. Planting aquatic seeds is another adventure, where kids learn about germination and growth. Sprinkle seeds over the substrate, gently cover them, and watch as they sprout into a carpet of green over the following weeks. Each step is a lesson in responsibility and observation, turning abstract concepts into tangible results.

Encouraging creativity through personalized projects is where the magic truly happens. Kids can design themed tanks that reflect their personalities, using favorite toys or characters as inspiration. Imagine a tank where dinosaurs roam among the plants, or one where superheroes keep watch over the fish. The possibilities are as limitless as their imaginations. Colorful gravel and decorations add flair, allowing young aquarists to express themselves while learning about color and composition.

Success stories abound, with young aquarists crafting their unique setups. Take, for example, Alex, who transformed a simple tank into an underwater pirate adventure, complete with a sunken ship and treasure chest. Or consider Lucy, whose fairy garden aquascape features miniature bridges and tiny mushrooms, a whimsical world where aquatic fairies might just dwell. Parents rave about the learning experience, praising the projects for sparking curiosity and fostering a love of science and nature. These projects aren't just about creating beautiful tanks; they're about empowering kids to explore, experiment, and express themselves, building confidence along with their aquariums.

Visual Element: Kid's Aquascaping Gallery

Aquascaping isn't just a hobby, it's an art form that grows and changes. One of the best ways to help kids feel proud of their hard work is by creating a Kid's Aquascaping Gallery, a special place to capture and celebrate their aquarium designs.

Why Create a Gallery?

A gallery allows children to:

- **See how far they've come** by looking back at earlier designs.

- Celebrate their creativity with friends and family.

- **Build confidence** by recognizing their improvements.

- **Stay motivated** to continue learning and trying new ideas.

It becomes a **visual diary** of their journey as young aquarists, helping them reflect on what they've learned about design, fish care, and aquatic life.

How to Build Your Gallery

1. **Take Photos of Each Creation** Encourage kids to take clear, well-lit photos of their aquarium every time they rearrange plants, add decorations, or complete a themed setup. *Tip: Take photos from different angles to capture all the details!*

2. Create a Digital Album or Scrapbook.

   - **Digital Album:** Use a phone, tablet, or computer to save and organize the pictures. You can even add captions or notes about what they changed or learned with each new layout.

   - **Physical Scrapbook:** Print the photos and create a scrapbook with spaces for writing dates, names for fish, or funny stories about their aquarium adventures.

3. **Add Captions and** Reflections help children write a sentence or two about what they love most about each design or what they might try differently next time. This builds observation skills and self-reflection.

4. **Share with Family and** Friends display the album at home or share photos

digitally with family members. This gives kids a chance to show off their hard work and feel proud of their efforts.

Make It Tradition

Encourage kids to update their gallery regularly as their skills grow. Over time, they'll build a personal collection of memories that celebrates their creativity, learning, and love for aquatic life.

Visual Appeal: Designing Child-Friendly Aquascapes

Visualize stepping into a room where a brightly colored aquarium immediately catches your eye, like a candy store window full of treats. Vibrant, eye-popping designs attract young aquarists, and aquascaping provides the perfect canvas for their colorful imaginations. Picture tanks brimming with radiant plants in neon greens and fiery reds, each leaf waving like a friendly hello. These splashes of color aren't just visually appealing; they capture the excitement and curiosity of young minds, making every glance into the tank an adventure. But why stop at plants? Add in decorations that tell a story—tiny pirate ships sailing through the sea, or castles where fish play the role of knights guarding their watery kingdom. These elements transform the tank into more than a habitat; they become a living storybook, enticing children to peer in and dream up tales of underwater escapades.

To create a tank that truly captivates, it's all about contrast and movement. Consider using contrasting colors to make your aquarium pop. Imagine a backdrop of deep blue against which vibrant orange fish dart back and forth, like flames dancing on water. This contrast not only draws the eye but also highlights the natural beauty of the aquatic world. Incorporating interactive elements like bubble makers takes the experience to another level. Picture bubbles rising to the surface, creating a whimsical, magical atmosphere that mesmerizes both kids and adults alike. These bubbles are like the aquarium's own applause, adding life and movement, and encouraging children to engage with their aquatic friends as they watch the bubbles rise and burst.

Now, let's talk about themes that spark imagination. How about an ocean adventure, where small submarines navigate through a sea teeming with playful sea creatures? Decorate the tank with miniature submarines and schools of fish that swim alongside, creating a sense of exploration and discovery. Or perhaps a fairy garden, where tiny bridges and mushrooms provide a fairytale landscape for fish to flit through like winged sprites? These themes transport kids to other worlds, where their imaginations can run wild and anything is possible. Themed tanks not only make for captivating displays but also serve as conversation starters, sparking curiosity and questions about the natural world.

Captivating aquascapes isn't just for show they're a source of inspiration and creativity. Consider the young aquarist who transformed a tank into a bustling coral reef, complete with colorful coral replicas and schools of vibrant fish. The result was a stunning display of life and color, a miniature ecosystem that captured the essence of the ocean. Or take the child who designed a whimsical forest scene, with driftwood branches reaching like gnarled trees and fish weaving through the shadows like woodland creatures. These setups offer a glimpse into the boundless creativity of young minds, proving that with a little imagination, an aquarium can become a window to any world they can dream up.

Visual Element: Step-by-Step Guide for a Themed Aquascape

Create Your Own Pirate Ship Themed Aquascape

A Step-by-Step Guide for Kids and Families

Bringing imagination to life is one of the most exciting parts of aquarium keeping! In this themed aquascape guide, you'll create a **pirate adventure scene** complete with ships, treasure chests, and ocean plants. Follow these simple steps to design your very own underwater masterpiece.

What You'll Need:

    1. An **aquarium** (10 to 20 gallons is ideal for beginners)

2. Pirate-themed decorations (such as ships, treasure chests, and caves)

3. Aquatic plants (like Java Fern, Anubias, or artificial plants)

4 Fish (such as guppies, tetras, or cory catfish)

5. Gravel or sand for the aquarium floor

6. Aquarium light and filter

7. Water conditioner to make tap water safe for fish

Step-by-Step Setup

Step 1: Choose Your Tank

Select a **10 to 20-gallon aquarium**—just the right size for your fish and decorations.

Step 2: Add the Substrate

Pour in **gravel or sand** to create your ocean floor. Smoothing it out makes it easier to place decorations.

Step 3: Place Your Pirate Decor

Add your **pirate ship, treasure chests**, and other fun decorations. Be sure to leave open space for your fish to swim freely.

Step 4: Add Plants for Extra Life

Plant life **or artificial aquatic plants** to complete your scene. Place taller plants in the back and smaller ones in the front to add depth and make your pirate world look alive.

Step 5: Fill with Water

Slowly fill your tank with **clean, treated water**. Always add **water conditioner** to remove chlorine and make it safe for your fish.

Step 6: Set Up Your Equipment

Install your **filter and aquarium light** to keep the water clean and your scene well-lit.

Step 7: Add Your Fish

Choose **peaceful fish** that match the size of your tank and enjoy watching them explore their new pirate adventure home.

You Did It!

You've just created your very own **pirate ship themed aquascape**! Encourage kids to name their fish and decorations, tell stories about their underwater pirates, and take care of their new aquatic friends.

Encouraging Responsibility: Teaching Kids Aquarium Maintenance

Envision a bustling underwater metropolis, where fish glide through their watery streets and plants sway like city trees in the current. This aquatic world doesn't run itself, though. It requires regular maintenance, like a well-oiled machine, to keep everything running smoothly. Now, picture your child as the mayor of this vibrant city, learning the ropes of responsibility through the care of their aquarium. It's not just about keeping the tank clean; it's about understanding the impact of their actions on this miniature ecosystem and realizing that even the smallest tasks can lead to big effects.

Daily feeding routines become an exercise in mindfulness. Your young aquarists will learn the importance of feeding the right amount, avoiding overfeeding, which can lead to a tank messier than a teenager's bedroom. They'll become keen observers, noticing when their fish are acting like they're auditioning for a drama, with strange swimming or unusual behavior. These observations are crucial, offering the first clues that something might be amiss. It's like being a detective in a mystery novel, piecing together clues to keep the peace in their underwater city.

For younger children, tasks like feeding and observing fish can be both manageable and rewarding. They're simple yet essential, fostering a sense of routine and care. Older kids undefined can dive into more complex tasks like assisting with water changes and cleaning. It's a step up in responsibility, akin to moving from a tricycle to a bicycle. They'll learn to handle equipment, measure water levels, and even understand basic water chemistry. These tasks not only teach practical skills but also instill a sense of accomplishment and pride in their growing capabilities.

Creating a maintenance schedule for kids can be a fun and engaging way to keep them organized. Visual charts with colorful stickers or magnets can outline daily, weekly, and monthly tasks, transforming maintenance into a game. Imagine a reward system where consistent participation earns points towards a new tank decoration or a special outing. It's like turning chores into a treasure hunt, where diligence and effort lead to exciting rewards. This approach not only keeps kids on track but also makes the learning process enjoyable and motivating.

Stories of young aquarists taking charge of their tanks are plentiful and inspiring. Take Emma, for instance, a ten-year-old who transformed her aquarium maintenance routine into a family affair. She created a colorful chart that hung proudly in the kitchen, marking off tasks each week with her trusty red pen. Her parents noted that Emma's confidence grew alongside her responsibility as she took pride in her role as the aquarium caretaker. Then there's Jack, a budding aquarist whose curiosity led him to discover a love for biology and chemistry through his interactions with the tank. His parents watched as he eagerly shared his newfound knowledge at school, teaching classmates about the fascinating world beneath the water's surface.

These stories highlight the profound impact that aquarium maintenance can have on young minds. They teach responsibility, nurture curiosity, and provide valuable life lessons that extend far beyond the glass walls of a tank. Parents have shared insights into how this hobby fosters growth and independence, revealing that it's not just the fish that flourish—it's the children too. With each task, your young aquarists learn that caring for a living ecosystem is both a privilege and a responsibility, one that they can manage with growing confidence and enthusiasm.

Conservation Education: Instilling Environmental Awareness

Picture this: a kid, wide-eyed, staring into an aquarium teeming with colorful fish and swaying plants. What they might not realize is that this small tank is a miniature version of the world's oceans and rivers bursting with life. Aquariums aren't just about the pretty fish and decor; they're gateways to understanding the bigger picture—our planet's ecosystems and the vital role they play. Through the lens of an aquarium, kids can learn about biodiversity, the interconnected web of life where each fish, plant, and rock plays a part. It's like understanding that every ingredient in a pizza has its role—take one away, and the whole thing falls apart. Sustainable practices in aquarium keeping can have a ripple effect on marine life. By choosing eco-friendly options and being mindful of resource use, we can teach kids that even small actions in their aquariums can contribute to a healthier planet.

Engaging kids in activities that emphasize environmental care can be both fun and enlightening. Picture them creating posters about endangered fish species, highlighting the challenges these creatures face in the wild. This isn't just an art project; it's a way for kids to connect with the world beyond their tank, turning facts and figures into a personal mission. Organizing community clean-up events transforms them into environmental superheroes, where the mission is to clear litter and save the day. These activities instill a sense of responsibility and empowerment, showing kids they can make a tangible difference, even if it's just by picking up a piece of trash.

But why stop there? Encouraging participation in broader conservation initiatives can amplify their impact. Local aquarium clubs focused on sustainability provide a platform for young aquarists to learn and share ideas. It's like a club meeting where the main agenda is saving the planet, one fish at a time. Supporting conservation organizations through fundraising opens the door to involvement in real-world efforts, teaching kids the power of collective action. From bake sales to fun runs, these activities not only raise funds but also raise awareness, turning each dollar into a vote for a healthier environment.

Success stories abound, offering a glimpse of what's possible when young minds embrace conservation. Take the inspiring tale of a group of kids who led a local river clean-up, armed with nets, gloves, and a mission to make a difference. Their efforts not only cleared debris but also sparked a community-wide movement, showing that when kids lead, adults follow. Or consider a school program that integrated aquariums into environmental studies, using them as living laboratories to explore topics like pollution and habitat loss. Students not only learned about ecosystems, but also took part in projects that directly benefited local conservation efforts. These stories highlight the incredible potential of conservation education, where young advocates emerge as leaders, driven by a passion for preserving the natural world.

Aquariums aren't just fish tanks; they're opportunities. They teach kids to see the world through a lens of stewardship and sustainability, where every action, no matter how small, contributes to a larger cause. By engaging them in activities that promote conservation, we nurture a generation that values our planet and its diverse life forms, ready to take on the challenges of tomorrow with knowledge and compassion.

Building a Family Hobby: Involving Everyone in Aquarium Care

An aquarium has more than a glass box filled with water and fish—it's a lively hub where families gather to laugh, learn, and bond. Picture this: Mom's fascinated by the vibrant fish, Dad's pondering filter systems like he's engineering a space shuttle, and the kids? They're overjoyed, placing decorations and naming every creature like they're part of the family. Aquariums can be miraculous family projects, offering opportunities for shared learning experiences that feel less like chores and more like adventures. It's not just about keeping fish alive; it's about cultivating a living art piece together—one that requires teamwork, patience, and a good dose of humor when things don't go as planned (like when that snail you swore was a rock starts moving).

Engaging every family member in aquarium care can be as easy as assigning tasks based on interests and abilities. Got a techie teen? Set them loose on setting up the tank's lighting system. Little ones can be the official fish feeders, their eyes wide with the responsibility of keeping their aquatic friends well-fed. Meanwhile, someone with a knack for design might take charge of arranging plants and rocks, creating a stunning underwater landscape. You could even plan family outings to aquarium stores or exhibits, turning a simple shopping trip into an exciting educational experience. These outings can spark fascinating conversations, with everyone sharing ideas and preferences, deciding together like a miniature board meeting over which fish to add next.

Communication is key to making aquarium care a cohesive family endeavor. Consider holding regular family meetings to discuss the aquarium's progress. These powwows can be as informal as a chat over dinner, with everyone sharing their observations and ideas. Encourage each family member to voice their thoughts—whether it's about trying a new plant species or adjusting the feeding schedule. You might even create a family blog or scrapbook about your aquarium adventures. Documenting the journey can be a creative outlet and a wonderful way to look back on how far you've come. Plus, it's a great excuse to show off those dazzling fish photos everyone keeps taking.

Families across the globe have found joy, and connection through shared aquarium projects. Take the Johnsons, for example—a family of four who transformed their dining room into an aquatic paradise. Every Saturday, they gather around the tank, each with a task: Dad checks the water chemistry, Mom trims the plants, and the kids eagerly feed their finned friends. They've even started a scrapbook, filled with photos and notes about their favorite fish moments. The project strengthened their bond, turning what began as a simple hobby into a cherished family tradition.

Aquariums offer a unique way to bring families together, encouraging collaboration, communication, and a shared sense of accomplishment. Whether you're designing an aquascape or troubleshooting a filter issue, every step is an opportunity to learn and grow together. And, you'll create not just a vibrant aquatic ecosystem, but also a tapestry of memories. Each water change, each new fish, a thread in the story of your family's aquarium adventure. As we wrap up this chapter, remember that the heart of the aquarium keeping is family, where every splash and bubble echoes with laughter and love.

"Quick Recap: Healthy Tank Habits"

ESSENTIAL STEPS FOR HEALTHY AQUARIUM

WATER PARAMETERS

WATER CHANGES
Change 20-20% of the water every 1-2 weeks using a siphon.

RINSE FILTER MEDIA
Gently rinse sponge or cartridge filter in tankwater (never tap).

CLEAN FILTERS
Clean of replace the filter medio according to the manufactur's instructions.

CLEAN PARAMETERS

WATCH FOR SIGNS OF STRESS
Watch for signs of stress, disease, or algae bloom.

RINSE FILTER MEDIA
Gently rinse, spenge / cafridge filter in tank, water (never tap).

FILTRATION

CLEAN ORI LAS BANC FILTER
Clean or replace the filter media according to manufacturer's instructions

CONTROL ALGAE GROWTH
Regularly remove excess algae to keep the tank clean.

COMMON PROBLEMS

WATER PARAMETERS

NON-SCRATCH

CONTROL ALGAE GROWTH

Regularly remove excess algoe to keep the tank clean.

Follow these simple habits each week to keep your tank clean, your fish stress-free, and your water parameters balanced.

Chapter 8: Cultivating Lifelong Learning: Beyond the Basics

Advanced Techniques,
Community Connections, and
Inspiration to Keep Growing as
a Passionate Aquarist

Picture this: You've conquered the basics of aquarium keeping, your fish are swimming happily, and your plants are flourishing. Now, you're staring at your tank, itching for something more. You want to dive into the deep end of aquascaping, where the water's fine, but the techniques are a little more complex. Welcome to advanced aquascaping, where your aquarium becomes not just a habitat, but a canvas for your creativity. It's like moving from finger painting to the fine art of Picasso, only with fewer berets and more algae scrapers.

Advanced aquascaping is where design meets science, and your tank transforms into a masterpiece of aquatic art. Let's talk about negative space, the unsung hero of sophisticated design. It's not just the absence of stuff; it's the strategic use of emptiness to highlight the elements you have. Think of it as the dramatic pause in a good joke—without it, the punchline just doesn't land. By using negative space effectively, you give your aquascape room to breathe, allowing each element to shine without overwhelming the senses. It's about restraint, which, if we're honest, can be tough when you're bursting with ideas.

Next, we wade into the waters of advanced hardscape manipulation. This isn't just about plopping a rock here or a piece of driftwood there. It's about creating a dynamic, flowing composition that guides the viewer's eye, telling a story with every curve and contour. Picture yourself as an underwater architect, sculpting the landscape with precision and flair. Advanced techniques might involve stacking rocks to create dramatic cliffs or weaving driftwood into intricate shapes. It's like playing an elaborate game of Jenga, but with less risk of everything toppling over.

Of course, no advanced aquascape is complete without rare plants and specialized substrates. High-light, CO2-demanding plants like Rotala and Anubias are the divas of the plant world. They require a bit more attention, but reward you with vibrant colors and lush growth. It's like having a high-maintenance pet that occasionally demands a spa day totally worth it for the aesthetic payoff. Pair these plants with layered substrates, like ADA Aquasoil, which provides a nutrient-rich environment perfect for root growth. It's like laying the red carpet for your plant stars, ensuring they have everything they need to take center stage.

For inspiration, look no further than the world of competitive aquascaping. International competitions showcase jaw-dropping designs that push the boundaries of creativity. Analyzing award-winning aquascapes reveals common themes, like the harmonious use of color and texture or the clever interplay of light and shadow. Renowned aquascapers often employ techniques like the Iwagumi style, a minimalist approach using a few carefully chosen stones to create a Zen-like balance. It's all about simplicity and serenity, a refreshing contrast to the chaos of everyday life.

If you're itching to try your hand at these advanced techniques, here's a step-by-step project to get you started: an Iwagumi-style layout. Begin with a clean slate, your tank empty and ready for transformation. Choose three key stones, the stars of your show, and arrange them in a triangular formation, with the largest stone as the focal point. Surround them with smaller rocks to create depth and realism, ensuring everything feels cohesive. Plant clusters of grass-like Eleocharis in the gaps, mimicking the soft, rolling hills of a Japanese landscape. It's like creating a miniature mountain range, right in your own living room.

For those with a taste for the colorful and complex, consider crafting a Dutch aquascape. This style embraces a riot of plant species, each contributing to a tapestry of color and form. Start by selecting a variety of plants with different heights and textures, arranging them in rows to create a sense of order amidst the chaos. Use foreground plants like Staurogyne reopens to carpet the front, while taller species like Ludwigia peruensis add drama at the back. Keep the layout balanced, with pops of color drawing the eye across the scene. It's a bit like choreographing a dance, where every plant has its part, and together they create a harmonious whole.

Visual Element: Mastering the Iwagumi Style

Bring balance, simplicity, and beauty to your aquarium by exploring the **Iwagumi Style**—a Japanese-inspired layout that uses carefully placed stones and minimal plants to create a peaceful, Zen-like underwater landscape.

Step 1: Understand the Iwagumi Layout

In Iwagumi, the stones are the stars of the show. You'll typically use:

- One large "Main Stone" (called *Oyaishi*) placed slightly off-center and tilted to create natural tension.

- Two or smaller "Supporting Stones" (*Fukuishi*) complemented the key stone and provide balance.

Visualization Tip: Picture a gentle mountain range rising from an open valley. Keep some space in the front for a clean, minimalist feel.

Step 2: Select Your Plants

People commonly use low-growing carpet plants in Iwagumi to enhance the natural landscape. Consider:

- Dwarf Hairgrass

- Monte Carlo

- Glossostigma

- Anubias Nana Petite (optional)

Take a moment to decide which plants you'd like to feature in your layout.

Step 3: Plan Your Lighting

Strong. Bright lighting is essential to support healthy plant growth in an Iwagumi aquascape. Choose an appropriate light for your tank and plan for about 6 to 8 hours of light per day.

Example lighting options include:

- LED aquarium lighting (energy efficient and plant-friendly)

- Fluorescent lighting (for broader tank coverage)

- Make sure your lighting schedule is consistent to avoid algae overgrowth.

Step 4: Reflect and Visualize

As you build your layout, ask yourself: "What feeling do I want to create in my aquarium?" Peaceful? Natural? Bold? Minimalist? Write it down or keep it in mind as your guiding vision.

Bringing It All Together

Use this guide as a reference while you design. Remember:

- Keep it simple.

- Balance your stones.

- Choose plants that complement, not clutter.

- Use lighting to bring the scene to life.

By following these principles, you'll create a stunning Iwagumi-style aquascape that brings a touch of Zen and natural harmony to your home.

Breeding Basics: Encouraging Fish Reproduction in Your Tank

So, you've mastered keeping fish alive, and now you're thinking about adding the title of "Breeder Extraordinaire" to your aquarium résumé. Breeding fish isn't just about sticking two fish together and hoping they'll get along like a couple on a reality dating show. It's more like orchestrating a The first step is creating a breeding tank. These tanks are like honeymoon suites for fish, where the magic happens. Choose a tank size based on the species you aim to breed, and make sure it's equipped with all the essentials: a gentle filter to prevent eggs from being swept away, and plenty of hiding spots for the shy couple.

Understanding fish breeding behaviors is crucial, as fish are surprisingly picky about their romantic environment. Some fish, like cichlids, are the doting parents of the aquatic world, known for their distinct parental care. They need a peaceful, stress-free setting to get in the mood. On the other hand, guppies are the prolific breeders of the fish realm, often needing little encouragement to multiply. They're like the rabbits of the aquarium world, always ready for love. Identifying triggers like changes in water temperature or light can help set the scene for these underwater love stories.

When choosing species for your first breeding attempt, guppies are a safe bet. These livebearers are easy to breed and require minimal intervention. Plus, their vibrant colors make for a visually appealing tank. If you're feeling adventurous, try your hand at breeding cichlids. Their intricate courtship rituals and parental instincts provide both a challenge and a reward. Watching cichlid parents guard their fry is like watching a soap opera unfold in your aquarium, complete with drama and unexpected plot twists.

Once the fish lay eggs or give birth to fry, the actual work begins. Raising fry successfully is all about providing the right conditions and diet. Think of fry as tiny, finned teenagers—they eat a lot and need their space. Feeding them requires a specialized diet, starting with tiny foods like liquid egg yolks or crushed fish flakes. As they grow, gradually introduce live foods to ensure their development. Protecting fry from larger tank mates is also crucial. Consider using a nursery tank or tank dividers to give them a safe space to grow.

Successful breeding setups can vary from community tanks with breeding pairs to dedicated breeding tanks designed for specific species. Some breeders have found success with community setups, where breeding pairs coexist with other species, providing a dynamic environment for fry development. These setups are like bustling neighborhoods where every fish has its role. Dedicated breeding tanks offer controlled conditions tailored to the specific needs of breeding fish. These tanks are akin to private nurseries, with every detail optimized for fry survival.

Take, for instance, the story of Lisa, an aquarist who set up a dedicated breeding tank for her angelfish. By carefully monitoring water parameters and providing ample hiding spots, she successfully raised a batch of healthy fry. Or consider Mark, who opted for a community setup with his guppies, allowing them to breed naturally while still maintaining a vibrant tank. These stories highlight the diverse approaches to breeding, each with its own challenges and rewards. Breeding fish is like solving a fascinating puzzle—each piece, from the tank set up to the species choice, contributes to the overall picture. So, whether you're dreaming of a guppy parade or a cichlid drama, with the right preparation and a dash of patience, you can turn your aquarium into a thriving nursery.

Joining the Community: Clubs, Forums, and Social Media

So, your knee-deep in aquarium gravel, and you've got more questions than fish in your tank. Where do you turn? Welcome to the world of aquarium communities, where everyone speaks fish and you're never judged for spending your Saturday night debating the merits of LED lighting. Engaging with the aquarium community isn't just about getting advice on why your guppies are staging a hunger strike. It's about diving into a pool of shared experiences and learning from people who've likely made the same rookie mistakes you have. Imagine having a team of aquatic experts at your fingertips, ready to share their secrets and maybe even a few horror stories of tanks gone wrong. It's like finding a virtual family that understands why you insist on talking about your fish like they're your children.

Connecting with fellow enthusiasts opens doors to collaboration and shared projects you might never have dreamed of tackling alone. Maybe you'll team up with a local club to build a community fish tank in a school, or join forces online to create a virtual showcase of your best aquascapes. The possibilities are endless, and the friendships you forge can be just as colorful and diverse as the fish you keep. You'll find yourself inspired by the collective creativity and innovation that flourishes when hobbyists come together, each bringing unique insights and experiences to the table.

Now, where do you find these mythical communities? Start with local aquarium clubs. They're like the secret societies of the fish world, but with less mystery and more potluck dinners. Check out community bulletin boards, pet stores, or even Facebook groups to find one near you. Attend a meeting, and a world where everyone understands the struggle of finding the perfect tank mate for that picky angelfish will welcome you. For those who prefer the comfort of their own couch, online forums and discussion boards are a treasure trove of information and camaraderie. Sites like FishForums.net are bustling with discussions on everything from breeding tips to tank setups, offering a platform for you to ask questions, share your own experiences, and learn from seasoned aquarists without ever leaving your living room.

Contributing to these discussions is where the real magic happens. Share your own fish tales, both the triumphs and the blunders. There's no shame in admitting that time you accidentally turned your tank into a frothy bubble bath because you went a little overboard with the soap. Your honesty might just help another newbie avoid a similar fate. Ask questions, no matter how silly they might seem, and don't be afraid to seek feedback on your latest aquascaping masterpiece. Your tank might just become the next viral sensation or at least earn you a few virtual high-fives from fellow hobbyists.

Consider the story of Jenny, a novice aquarist who joined her local club and quickly became a regular at meetings. Through her involvement, she learned advanced breeding techniques and even collaborated on a community project to set up a tank at a local library. Or take Mike, who found his niche on an online forum, where his witty posts and quirky tank designs have made him a beloved character in the community. His insightful advice and humorous anecdotes keep fellow members coming back for more, turning what was once a solitary hobby into a vibrant social experience.

So, whether you're attending meetings in person or logging into forums from the comfort of your couch, joining the aquarium community is like finding your people. You'll discover a network of support and encouragement, where everyone understands the joys and challenges of keeping fish. It's a place where you can grow and learn, sharing your passion with others who are just as fish-obsessed as you are.

Staying Informed: Resources for Continuous Learning

Picture this: you're standing in front of your aquarium, admiring your aquatic masterpiece, when suddenly, the algae throws a wild party. Or your prized fish does the backstroke—unfortunately, not by choice. Panic sets in, but fret not! Staying informed is the key to keeping your underwater world from turning into a soap opera. There's a universe of resources out there to keep you on top of your fishkeeping game. Comprehensive books are a treasure trove of wisdom, covering everything from the intricacies of water chemistry to the subtle art of aquascaping. Titles like "The Complete Aquarium Guide" or "The Encyclopedia of Aquarium and Pond Fish" offer in-depth insights into specific topics. Whether you're a newbie trying to figure out why your goldfish looks grumpy, or a seasoned aquarist curious about the latest in CO2 injection techniques, there's a book with your name on it.

But books aren't the only way to reel in knowledge. The digital age has blessed us with online courses and webinars that dive deep into niche topics. Websites like Coursera and Udemy host classes on everything from basic fish care to advanced aquascaping techniques. These virtual classrooms bring together experts and enthusiasts from around the globe, offering a smorgasbord of information that you can digest at your leisure, no scuba gear required. It's like having a team of aquatic gurus ready to spill their secrets at the click of a mouse.

Now, let's talk about science because who doesn't love an excellent paper on fish behavior while sipping coffee? Scientific journals and publications are the unsung heroes of aquarium learning. They provide a wealth of research on fish ecology and behavior, offering insights that can transform your aquarium practices. Want to know why your angelfish are reenacting West Side Story in your tank? Studies on territorial behaviors might just hold the answer. Applying these findings to your personal setups can be like adding a turbo boost to your fishkeeping skills, turning you into the Einstein of aquariums.

Keeping up with industry trends is crucial, too. Aquarium magazines and newsletters will keep you up-to-date. These publications often feature the latest innovations, from eco-friendly filtration systems to the hottest new fish species. They're like the gossip columns of the aquarium world, only with more fins and less drama. Following influential aquarists on social media is another great way to stay current. Platforms like Instagram and YouTube are brimming with creators who share tips, tricks, and sometimes just really adorable fish photos. It's an endless stream of inspiration and learning, all from the comfort of your favorite armchair.

Take inspiration from lifelong learners in the hobby. Meet Sarah, who attends international conferences to soak up the latest in aquarium technology and design. Her tanks are a testament to the ever-evolving nature of the hobby, each setup more innovative than the last. Or consider Jake, whose fascination with fish behavior led him down a rabbit hole of scientific papers. His tanks are a living lab, each one a testament to his dedication to applying new knowledge. These individuals remind us that the aquarium hobby isn't just about keeping fish alive—it's about cultivating a passion for learning and discovery.

Staying informed is not just about acquiring knowledge; it's about feeding your curiosity and allowing your hobby to grow alongside it. As you explore these resources, you'll find that each new piece of information adds another layer to your understanding, turning your aquarium from a mere fish tank into a vibrant ecosystem teeming with life and possibility.

Experimenting with New Techniques: Overcoming the Fear of Mistakes

So, you've got your aquarium looking pretty snazzy, but there's a nagging itch to shake things up a bit. Maybe you're eyeing that pile of driftwood, wondering if it would look better as a gravity-defying sculpture. Or perhaps you're tempted to see what happens if you try a low-water setup, just for kicks. Experimentation in aquarium keeping is like adding a pinch of spice to your culinary creations—sometimes the result is deliciously unexpected, and other times, well, let's just say it's a learning experience. Trying unconventional aquascape designs can transform your tank from a safe, predictable setup to a jaw-dropping wonderland. Whether you're stacking rocks in a way that defies physics or creating a labyrinth of plant roots, pushing the boundaries of traditional aquascaping can lead to stunning results. It's like crafting an underwater fairy tale, where every stone and plant tells a part of the story.

Of course, with great experimentation comes the occasional hiccup. Maybe the water turns a peculiar shade of green, or your fish give you the side-eye. These setbacks are superb opportunities. They teach you more than any guidebook ever could. Analyzing what went wrong—was it the lighting, the substrate, or just an overexcited imagination? Provides insights that help you refine your approach. It's like getting a backstage pass to your own aquarium mistakes, allowing you to see the mechanics of what didn't quite work and how to fix it. Adapting methods based on experiences is like building a toolbox of knowledge, each mistake adding another tool to your kit.

To minimize risks while trying new techniques, consider setting up temporary test tanks. Think of them as rehearsal stages where you can play out your most daring ideas without the pressure of a full-scale production. They're perfect for testing new water management techniques or experimenting with that wild aquascape layout you've been dreaming of. Documenting these experiments is also crucial. Keep a journal or take photos to track changes and outcomes. It's like being a scientist in your own home, gathering data and drawing conclusions to inform future projects.

New ideas often come from people who are creative and think differently. Take, for instance, the aquarist who pioneered a method of breeding fish using a rotating nursery tank system. By simulating a natural current, they created an environment that significantly increased fry survival rates. Or consider the visionary who challenged traditional norms by creating a vertical aquascape, stacking layers of substrate and plants in a column-like structure. The result was a mesmerizing waterfall effect, with fish darting through levels like an underwater skyscraper. These cases show that while not every experiment leads to a breakthrough, those that do can redefine what's possible.

In the world of aquariums, experimentation is the spark that drives innovation. It's the willingness to try something new, to mix and match ideas until you find a combination that sings. Whether you're testing a novel filtration system or trying your hand at a biotope recreation, embrace the unknown with enthusiasm. Remember, even the most seasoned experts started as curious novices, eager to try new things and learn from the inevitable bumps along the way. Get started, and let your imagination run wild.

Celebrating Success: Sharing Your Aquarium Experiences with Others

Visualize standing in front of your aquarium, watching your fish dart through the water like synchronized swimmers. You've come a long way from those initial hiccups, like the time your tank turned into a frothy soda fountain because you forgot to rinse the gravel. Recognizing these milestones is important. It's about more than just patting yourself on the back; it's about acknowledging the growth and learning that happened along the way. So, take a moment to reflect on how far you've come. Document your progress through photos and journals, creating a visual diary of your journey. Capture the transformation of your tank from a beginner's experiment into a thriving ecosystem. These records aren't just for nostalgia; they're a testament to your dedication and resilience.

Sharing your experiences can inspire others, turning your personal achievements into a beacon of inspiration. Consider presenting your story at local aquarium clubs or hosting an online webinar. Tell the tale of your tank's evolution, complete with the ups, the downs, and the occasional sideways. Your story might encourage someone else who's knee-deep in algae and doubt to keep going. If public speaking isn't your thing, write about your experiences. Contribute articles or blog posts to aquarium magazines or online platforms. Your words can reach a broader audience, offering insights and encouragement to fellow aquarists around the globe. Someone might find inspiration in your candid account of accidentally introducing a snail army to your pristine aquascape.

Feedback and recognition from others can also enhance your satisfaction and learning. Taking part in aquarium competitions can be a thrilling way to showcase your work and receive constructive feedback. It's not just about winning; it's about the camaraderie and learning that comes from being part of a community. Sharing tank updates on social media platforms can also garner positive reinforcement. Post photos of your latest aquascaping triumphs, and watch as fellow hobbyists chime in with likes, comments, and tips. This exchange of ideas and encouragement fosters a sense of belonging and motivation to continue refining your skills.

Consider the stories of aquarists who have shared their journeys with the world. Many have found their niche on social media, amassing followers who eagerly await each new tank update. These aquascapers have turned their passion into a source of inspiration and education for others. Take, for instance, Alex, whose vibrant and imaginative aquascapes have gained a dedicated online following. Through his posts, he shares not only his successes but also the challenges he faces, creating a relatable and motivating presence in the community. Or think of Maria, a reader who became a mentor to newcomers, offering guidance and support based on her own experiences. Her willingness to share her journey has inspired countless others to dive into the world of aquariums with confidence.

Celebrating success in the aquarium hobby isn't just about the destination; it's about acknowledging the journey. It's about sharing your story and learning from others, creating a vibrant tapestry of experiences and knowledge. As you continue to explore the depths of aquarium keeping, remember that each success, no matter how small, adds to the rich mosaic of your aquatic adventure. Embrace these moments and let them fuel your passion for the hobby as you forge ahead with new challenges and discoveries.

What's Next?

Your first tank is just the beginning. Explore, grow, and share your underwater passion with confidence.

There's always more to explore. Whether it's breeding guppies, building a new aquascape, or mentoring new hobbyists—you've got this.

Conclusion

Well, my friend, you've made it to the end of our aquatic adventure! Let's take a moment to reflect on the journey we've shared. Together, we've navigated the sometimes choppy, sometimes crystal-clear waters of freshwater aquarium keeping. We've explored the nooks and crannies of tank setup, dove into the colorful world of fish compatibility, and even dipped our toes into the art of aquascaping. It's been a wild ride, hasn't it?

Remember when we first started? The thought of setting up an aquarium might have seemed as daunting as swimming with sharks. But look at you now! Because: You possess the knowledge and skills to build a thriving underwater paradise. You know how to choose the perfect tank size, pick the right equipment, and even prevent those pesky algae blooms. You're practically a fish whisperer!

Let's not forget the most important lessons we've learned along the way. Foremost, always remember that your aquarium is a delicate ecosystem. It's like a tiny city where every inhabitant plays a role. Keep that balance in check, and your tank will flourish like a well-oiled machine. And speaking of inhabitants, you're now a pro at matching fish like an aquatic matchmaker. You know which species the life of the party and which ones are prefer a quieter corner of the tank.

Of course, even the most experienced aquarists make mistakes sometimes. However, my friend, this knowledge will help you avoid the most common pitfalls. You know that overfeeding your fish is like giving them an all-you-can-eat buffet—tempting, but ultimately not great for their waistline or your water quality. You understand that mixing incompatible fish is like trying to host a dinner party with feuding relatives—it's bound to end in chaos. And you know well that overcrowding your tank is like trying to fit too many clowns in a car—it might seem funny at first, but it's not sustainable in the long run.

But perhaps the most important lesson of all is to never stop learning. The world of aquariums is as vast and fascinating as the oceans themselves. There's always a new species to discover, a new aquascaping technique to try, or a new piece of equipment to geek out over. So keep exploring, experimenting, and keep growing your aquatic knowledge. Join a community of fellow enthusiasts, attend a conference or two, and don't be afraid to ask questions. After all, even the most experienced aquarists started somewhere.

As we wrap up this chapter of your aquarium journey, I want to take a moment to say thank you. Thank you for trusting me to guide you through this process, for sharing your passion and enthusiasm, and for being an incredible student. Watching you grow and learn has been as rewarding as watching a tiny fry transform into a majestic adult fish.

So, what's next for you? Well, that's the exciting part. Armed with the knowledge and skills you've gained, you're ready to dive into the world of aquariums with confidence. Whether you're setting up your first tank or revamping an existing one, you've got this. And remember, you're not alone. You're part of a vibrant community of aquarium enthusiasts, all eager to share their experiences and cheer you on.

As you embark on your next aquatic adventure, I encourage you to share your own stories. While: Setting up your tank, did you have a hilarious mishap? Did you witness an incredible moment between your fish? Did you create an aquascape that rivals the Sistine Chapel? We want to hear about it! Share your triumphs, your challenges, and everything in between. Because that's what this hobby is all about—learning, growing, and connecting with others who share your passion.

So here's to you, my friend. Here's to your future aquariums, filled with vibrant fish, lush plants, and endless possibilities. Here's to the joy, the wonder, and the occasional frustration that comes with being an aquarist. And most of all, here's the incredible journey you've embarked on. I can't wait to see where you take it.

References

- API Fish Care. (n.d.). Choosing the right aquarium size. API Fish Care. https://apifishcare.com/post/choosing-the-right-aquarium-size

- Fish Tanks Direct. (n.d.). Glass vs. acrylic aquarium: What is the difference? Fish Tanks Direct. https://fishtanksdirect.com/blog/glass-vs-acrylic-aquarium-what-is-the-difference/

- Blessings Aquarium. (n.d.). Budget aquariums: Setting up on a tight budget. Blessings Aquarium. https://www.blessingsaquarium.com/post/budget-aquariums

- Blessings Aquarium. (n.d.). Sustainable aquascaping: Eco-friendly practices for hobbyists. Blessings Aquarium. https://www.blessingsaquarium.com/post/sustainable-aquascaping-eco-friendly-practices-for-hobbyists

- Fish Tanks Direct. (n.d.). The art of aquascaping: Design principles and techniques. Fish Tanks Direct. https://fishtanksdirect.com/blog/art-of-aquascaping-design-principles-and-techniques/

- Aquascaping Love. (n.d.). The elements of aquascaping: Rocks, driftwood & substrates. Aquascaping Love. https://aquascapinglove.com/learn-aquascaping/elements-of-aquascaping-rocks-driftwood-substrates/

- Modern Aquarium. (n.d.). Top 10 live aquascaping plants for beginners. Modern Aquarium. https://www.modernaquarium.com/blog/top-10-live-aquascaping-plants-for-beginners/

- Aquasabi. (n.d.). Creating a three-dimensional layout with depth.

Sub. https://www.aquasabi.com/aquascaping-wiki_aquascaping_creating-a-three-dimensional-layout-with-a-pronounced-sense-of-depth

- Petco. (n.d.). Understanding the nitrogen cycle. Petco. https://www.petco.com/content/content-hub/home/articlePages/caresheets/nitrogen-cycle.html

- The Spruce Pets. (n.d.). The 16 best aquarium water test kits. The Spruce Pets. https://www.thesprucepets.com/aquarium-water-test-kits-1381915

- Atlas Scientific. (n.d.). How to lower the pH in a freshwater aquarium. Atlas Scientific. https://atlas-scientific.com/blog/how-to-lower-ph-in-freshwater-aquarium/

- Splashy Fish. (n.d.). Sustainable freshwater aquarium guide. Splashy Fish. https://splashyfishstore.com/blogs/all-thing-aquarium-related-blog/sustainable-freshwater-aquarium-guide

- The Spruce Pets. (n.d.). 11 easiest fish to take care of for new fish parents. The Spruce Pets. https://www.thesprucepets.com/low-maintenance-freshwater-fish-4770223

- LiveAquaria. (n.d.). Freshwater fish compatibility chart. LiveAquaria. https://www.liveaquaria.com/general/general.cfm?general_pagesid=539

- Chewy. (n.d.). Fish stress: Signs, causes, and treatment. Chewy. https://be.chewy.com/aquarium-fish-stress/

- Fishkeeper. (n.d.). Quarantining new fish: Why and how. Fish keeper. https://www.fishkeeper.co.uk/faq/do-i-need-to-quarantine-my-new-fish-and-if-so-how-do-i-do-it/

- Simplicity Aquatics. (n.d.). How to choose aquarium filter media: Mechanical filtration. Simplicity Aquatics. https://www.simplicityaquatics.com/blog/how-to-choose-aquarium-filter-media-mechanical-filtration/

- Blessings Aquarium. (n.d.). How to grow beneficial bacteria in aquarium. Blessings Aquarium. https://www.blessingsaquarium.com/post/grow-bacteria-in-aquarium

- FishLore Forum. (n.d.). DIY 5 gallon canister filter build. FishLore Forum. https://www.fishlore.com/aquariumfishforum/threads/diy-5-gallon-canister-filter-build.213840/

- Pet Me Daily. (n.d.). Aquarium filter not working: Common reasons and how to fix it. Pet Me Daily. https://petmedaily.com/aquarium-filter-not-working/

- The Spruce Pets. (n.d.). Routine aquarium maintenance. The Spruce Pets. https://www.thesprucepets.com/routine-aquarium-maintenance-1381084

- Merck Veterinary Manual. (n.d.). Disorders and diseases of fish. Merck Veterinary Manual. https://www.merckvetmanual.com/all-other-pets/fish/disorders-and-diseases-of-fish

- The Spruce Pets. (n.d.). How to control and prevent algae in your fish tank. The Spruce Pets. https://www.thesprucepets.com/aquarium-algae-1379979

- Aquarium Co-Op. (n.d.). How to properly clean your fish tank. Aquarium Co-Op. https://www.aquariumcoop.com/blogs/aquarium/aquarium-cleaning

- Study.com. (n.d.). Water chemistry: Lesson for kids. Study.com. https://study.com/academy/lesson/water-chemistry-lesson-for-kids.html

- Sixteen:Nine. (2023, October 26). Genuinely engaging and immersive projection exhibit for virtual aquariums. Sixteen:Nine. https://www.sixteen-nine.net/2023/10/26/genuinely-engaging-and-immersive-projection-exhibit-lets-kids-draw-color-fish-for-virtual-aquarium/

- Dustin's Fish Tanks. (n.d.). So, your kid wants a fish tank. Dustin's Fish Tanks. https://dustinsfishtanks.com/blogs/dustins-blog/kids-tanks

- HubPages. (n.d.). Educational benefits of aquarium care for kids. HubPages. https://discover.hubpages.com/animals/Aquarium-Care-for-Kids

- Fish Care 101. (n.d.). Advanced aquascaping guide: Creating and maintaining complex designs. Fish Care 101. https://www.fishcare101.com/reviews/fish-aquarium/advanced-aquascaping/

- WikiHow. (n.d.). Fish breeding: Basic mating instructions for beginners. WikiHow. https://www.wikihow.com/Breed-Fish

- FishForums.net. (n.d.). Fish forum: Tropical fish and aquarium community. FishForums.net. https://www.fishforums.net/

- Aqua Vim. (n.d.). Top 2023 home aquarium trends. Aqua Vim. https://aquavim.com/blogs/default-blog/top-2023-home-aquarium-trends

Leave A Review:

I hope this guide helped you feel confident and inspired to create a freshwater aquarium that brings you joy.

Why Your Review Matters:

- **It helps fellow hobbyists** discover this easy-to-follow guide.

- **It encourages me, Luna Wildheart,** to continue creating helpful resources for aquarium lovers like you.

- **It gives valuable feedback** for improving future editions.

Whether it's a quick comment or a detailed review, **your voice makes a difference**.

Scan & Share Your Experience

Use your phone's camera to scan the QR code below and leave your review in just a few clicks:

QR Code for Reviewers

Thank you again for your support, and happy fishkeeping! — **Luna Wildheart**